藍

JAPANESE INDIGO DESIGN
The collection of Sadako Fukui

京都書院／KYOTO SHOIN

Editor : Tomoe Ohmae

Translator : Kimiko Steiner

Photographer : Photo Apple One

Photographer's assistant : Nobuko Maruoka, Yoko Kondo, Ayako Kondo

JAPANESE INDIGO DESIGN
——— by Sadako Fukui ———

First Edition : January, 1992

Publisher : Mamoru Fujioka

Publishing office : Kyoto Shoin Co., Ltd.
　　　　　　　　　Sanjo-agaru, Horikawa
　　　　　　　　　Nakagyo-ku, Kyoto 604, Japan.

Printer : Daiyo Art Printing Co., Ltd.

Bookbindery : Dai-Nippon Bindery Co., Ltd.

©Sadako Fukui, 1991. Printed in Japan

ISBN4-7636-6045-4

CONTENTS

序・藍のデザイン／福井貞子 ……………… 4

染　SOME ……………… 10

縞　SHIMA ……………… 34

格子　KŌSHI ……………… 38

絣　KASURI ……………… 44

　絵画文様　Pictorial patterns ……………… 52

　幾何文様　Geometric patterns ……………… 84

藍のデザイン・・・

　江戸末期から明治にかけて、全国各地に独特の個性豊かな木綿絣が進展したが、中でも、西日本の久留米、伊予、備後、山陰地方(広瀬・弓浜・倉吉)の絣は有名だった。

　しかし、近年の大量機械生産や化学繊維の出現によって、山陰地方にも化繊の新製品が次第に波及するにつれて、紺一辺倒の木綿衣料の生活が崩れ、庶民の生活が非常にカラフルに軽々しくなった。新流行の波に乗り遅れまいとする風潮の中、木綿の染織品は廃物同様に処分されはじめ、化繊衣料がそれに取って変わった。

　そのころ(昭和35年ごろ)、私は古老に織物の手ほどきをうけていて、古絣を手本に、文様をセロハンで模写して型紙を作り、試行錯誤の繰り返しで絵絣を織り出した。当時は、染織デザイン書や技術に関する文献が入手できず、先人の遺作から学ぶしか方法がなかった。今まで、紺一色で愚鈍にさえみえていた紺絣の中、幾千万種の絵文様があることに気付き始めると、染織の技術を習得したいというささやかな願望が私の中で沸き起こってきた。やがてそれは、布の蒐集と聞き取り調査にまで広がり、私は日々小躍りし、嘆声を漏らしながら夢中になった。

　高度経済成長による農山村の衣食住の生活改善は急速に進み、すべての物を捨て去る恐るべき風潮が生まれた。祖先伝来の単笥や長持、家具調度品などが収められていた所蔵庫を、解体業者に処分を依頼して灰にする者もいる。このように、新生活への切り替えが錯覚され、在来の日本文化が否定され、消滅される傾向すらあった。私は、人が捨てようとする使い古しの物を、お金を出して買い上げたり新品と交換したりした。しかし、若年未熟の私は、布の命や価値に対する意識が希薄だったため、実物大の蒲団地や着物類、野良着は避け、部分的に切断したひと柄(図柄単位、約30㎝)を収集し、台紙に貼付し、製織年代・製織者・用途・名称と産地を記録して標本を作った。その後十年たって、かつて訪れた村々を再び歩いた時には、当時の老人の姿はなく、染織の遺品や工具もほとんどなくなっていた。古老たちが、それらを「形見に残してくれ」と切願したことが悔やまれて仕方がない。

　足を運び、聞き取り調査によって収集した布は、一枚一枚洗い清め整理を重ねていった。年代毎に量がまとまると、その時代の全体的な傾向も把握でき、藍の濃淡差や文様の精巧さによる生活レベルの差、文様の地域別傾向と特長、用途、モチーフ、技法、文様の変遷など、遺品が語りかけてくれるようになった。

　収集資料の多くは、天然繊維の麻や木綿を藍染めにしたデザインで、材質や色彩の制約を受けながら、その範囲内で各種の文様を自由に展開させている。個人差・性差・家族の自己表現を衣料に託す役割を担ったのは、文盲の女性たちである。厳しい労働の中にも、慎ましい美意識に満ちた生活がうかがえる。土地の山野で手軽に採集できる草木染、たとえば、楊梅皮や黄櫨など藍染めに重ねる色相が縞糸に織り込まれ陰の光沢を見せているなど、遺品についての解説も語り尽くせない。

資料の分類と整理集成、デザインなど、私の前には多岐にわたる研究の道が開かれた。と同時に私は、木綿文化の底無しの力量に改めて驚嘆する。染織のデザインは無限であり、四季折々の自然から学んだ花鳥山水や生活器具などが絵文や幾何文に表現されている。織り絣以前の染色の文様の模倣も見逃せないが、絣で描かれた幾何文様は、移行・反復・対称と数学的な展開を見せている。しかし、点と線・四角・三角・円の構成の多様な図形は、けして机上のデザインではなく、女性達の働きながらの発想から生まれたものである。在家の女性たちは、総デザイナーであったと言えよう。木綿と藍のデザインは、洗い晒すたびにより鮮明になる。外観の美しさだけではない。貧困と苦境の中で心を浄化させながら織り出した布の重量感には、愛と祈りが込められ、精神を鼓舞させる何かを宿している。女性の執念が、経糸と緯糸の交差する密度の中で、底光りとなっているように感じる。

　こうした各種のデザインは、麻や木綿の天然繊維の上に染め出され、縞や絣によって織り出され、蒲団・着物・外被・袖なし・下着類・風呂敷・袋物などに使われていた。私が収集した資料も、江戸末期から昭和二十年ごろ(1845〜1945年)までの、約百年間にわたる庶民の生活衣料が中心となっている。嫁入りの持参品、出産や成人祝いの際に織られたもの、野良着から外出着に至るまで多種多様である。

　本書には染、縞・格子、絣の三様に工程の異なるものを収めている。この三体は、個別に存在していたのではなく渾然と生活の中で溶け合っていたのである。染色は、白布に型紙をあて糊で防染して文様を出す。小紋や中型の型紙は繊細精密に彫られ、可能な限り高度な技術である。また手描き染めは、伸びやかに雄大に、筒描きにより絵文を表現している。縞・格子の工程は、あらかじめ縞計算をし、糸を染色し藍の濃淡を縞に配分して製織する。絵絣は、絵画文の型紙を白糸に置き、墨印をする。その糸を手括り防染作業によって絣糸を作り、絵文様を織出する。縞が粋な美しさであれば、絣の曲線絵文も味わい深い。しかし、染色の型紙より更にデザインを単純化し、製織工程の糸のかすれ、染液の浸透度を考慮して作図しなければ文様が潰れる。このような三体の工程上の特長を踏まえた上で、各種デザインを考察していただきたい。

　この度、京都書院の杉村卓二氏・大前朋恵氏、カメラマンの金谷英雄氏の御好意と御指導によって、庶民の衣料がデザイン書として編集され世に出る事になり喜びに堪えない。世界に誇りうる技術と文様として、今後ともこのデザインが生活の中で生かされ役立つことを念願すると共に、心から感謝を申し上げる。

1991年9月

福井貞子

Japanese indigo design

From the end of the Edo Period through the Meiji Period, a unique indigo dye cotton ikat (*kasuri* or splashed patterns) with individual, outstanding designs flourished throughout Japan. Among these works, those produced in the western part such as Kurume in Kyushu, Iyo in Shikoku, Hirose, Yumihama and Kurayoshi in the San'in area are especially known for their high quality.

Later, when machine-made materials began to be mass-produced and synthetic fibers appeared, these new products gradually penetrated into the people's lives. The hand-woven and hand-dyed cotton fabrics were replaced by the new mass-produced synthetic materials, and the traditional cloths were discarded. As a result, the clothing became more colorful and light.

Around 1960 I was studying weaving from an old weaver. Since no books on weaving or dying were available in those days, the only way I could learn about designs and techniques of ikat were from the remaining works of the past. So, I copied patterns of the old ikat on tracing paper, then make pattern sheets for weaving *e-gasuri* (picture ikat). I learned by trial and error.

After realizing there were countless numbers of patterns employed in this mono-color indigo textile, my orginal intention of simply mastering weaving and dyeing techniques expanded to include collecting the old cloth and information from weavers. I started to buy old, worn cloth which people were ready to throw away. Or sometimes I traded them for new materials. However, at that time, I was not fully aware of their value, nor did I have enough respect for the labor of the weavers. I was avoiding buying large, full-scale cloth, such as bed covers, *kimono* and peasant costumes. My main interest was merely to collect samples of patterns.

Therefore, instead of taking the entire cloth, I cut out one piece of the pattern (about 30cm square) from the whole material. Then I mounted it on paper and made a file of samples recording such information as the name of the weaver, the year of production, the place of production, the use of the cloth, and the style of the pattern. Ten years later, when I revisited those villages, most of the old people from whom I had bought had passed away. I could no longer see the old materials or tools. I deeply regret ignoring these old people's request to keep all the cloth that they had made as momentos of their lives.

The overall standard of living in the countryside has improved rapidly in keeping with Japan's recent economical growth, resulting in an embarrassing tendency to throw things away too casually. Chests of drawers, large, oblong traditional style chests and cabinets have been abandoned and replaced with tasteless new ones. People have even torn down their storehouses which had been handed down for many generations. The changes in the new lifestyle are made in the wrong direction, denying traditional Japanese culture. I have tried to preserve the lives of these disappearing objects as much as possible, but naturally for an individual there are financial and physical limits to collecting them all.

Each of the pieces I collected through visiting and interviewing the owners was washed, ironed and put into files. After a rather large number from the same period had been compiled, the overall characteristics became evident. Standards of people's lives were also reflected in the density of the dyed indigo colors and the degree of the elaborateness of the patterns. I became aware of the messege that each cloth carries: the trend and characteristics of the patterns made in each area, the use of the materials, motifs and techniques which changed through the ages.

Many of the collected fabrics are made of natural materials, either cotton or hemp dyed in indigo. In 1628, the Tokugawa Shogunate regulated the costumes each class could wear and inhibited ordinary people from wearing anything except indigo cotton or hemp. Within this restriction a great variety of patterns was created. The women who were in charge of the family clothing were illiterate. They took care of the apparel for the different ages, sexes and individual tastes of the family members. Regardless of their poverty and hard working conditions, they developed refined, aesthetic qualities. When I look at my collection, images of these women come to mind and I am quite moved.

Through compiling, classifying and analyzing these samples, I noticed that there are diverse ways open for the study of indigo fabrics. I was amazed at the rich and varied culture that cotton weaving had developed. The ikat designs vary almost infinitely.

Sadako Fukui

Seasonal portrayals of nature, such as landscapes, flowers and birds, and even daily utensils were depicted either figuratively or geometrically. Those which imitated the patterns of the old textiles before the appearance of ikat are attractive, but the geometrical patterns which developed into transformation, repetiton and symmetry are especially fascinating. These designs were not planned on desks but rather emerged spontaneously during the daily labor. Whenever some idea came to mind, the weavers jotted it down on a piece of paper. These diversified designs, composed of dots, lines, squares, triangles and circles, prove that these women were not merely simple craftspeople but, in fact, they were artistic designers.

The plants growing in the nearby fields and mountains were picked and used for coloring some part of the yarns. For instance, pigments extracted from such plants as *Myrica rubra* and *Phellodendron amurense* were applied to the pre-dyed warp to accentuate the indigo dyed materials. Also there are some cloths in which silk warp is partially employed bringing out a hidden glossy beauty. The techniques found in these exquisite materials are beyond our imagination.

These fabrics were used for bed covers, *kimono,* gowns, vests, undergarments, wrapping cloth, bags and pouches. My collection is composed of cloth produced over a span of one hundred years, from the end of the Edo Period to early Showa (1845-1945). From peasant costumes to street clothes, this collection includes an extensive range of materials. Many of them were items made for trousseau, or for special occasions like celebrating births or for coming-of-age ceremonies.

Every time indigo cotton is washed and bleached in the sun, the clarity and contrast of the colors increase. The fascinating beauty of indigo seems to be enhanced by the weaver's passion. When I touch the cloth, I can feel the love and prayers that the weavers had woven into the material, something which stimulates and inspires the spirit. I belive these women, in their poor and suffering conditions, tried to purify their minds by creating these cloths. Woman's deep emotion is alive within the intersecting density of warp and weft.

This book introduces three kinds of indigo textiles: paste resist dye cloth, ikat weaving, and stripe weaving, each of which employs a different process. These three kinds of materials were harmoniously woven into the lives of the ordinary people.

Paste resist dyeing employed two methods: *katazome* and *tsutsugaki*. *Katazome* requires a stencil cut into a design, which is placed on a white cloth. Paste is then applied through it onto the fabric before submerging it into the indigo tub. These stencils were cut into extremely elaborate designs demonstrating a highly technical craftsmanship. In the *tsutsugaki* method, the pattern is drawn by hand, with rice paste squeezed directly onto the fabric from a cone-shaped holder. This technique enables a free and bold depiction of the designs.

In the case of stripes, the length of the warp is figured out first and, according to the design of the stripes' color, each bundle of thread is dyed into different colors. In this way, subtle tones of indigo blue can be attained.

Ikat is made of yarn partially dyed by tying desired areas of the thread into bundles for resist dyeing before submerging into a dye bath. The *e-gasuri* (picture ikat) technique requires accurate calculation of the resist areas; therefore, a pattern sheet is employed for the markings. In order to have a clear design, the penetrating rate of the dye into the thread and the splashing effect should be carefully planned. When *e-gasuri* is combined with stripes, the beauty of the curving lines of ikat are enhanced by linear lines. When you look at the pictures in this book, please remember the forementioned characteristics of these processes.

I want to express my thanks to the editors of Kyoto Shoin Co., Ltd., Mr. Takuji Sugimura and Ms. Tomoe Ohmae, and also the photographer, Mr. Hideo Kanaya, for their kind guidance and cooperation to realize the publication of a textile design book by and for the ordinary people. I hope this book will be used daily by its readers.

September, 1991

JAPANESE INDIGO DESIGN

SOME; *Dyeing*

染

1

2

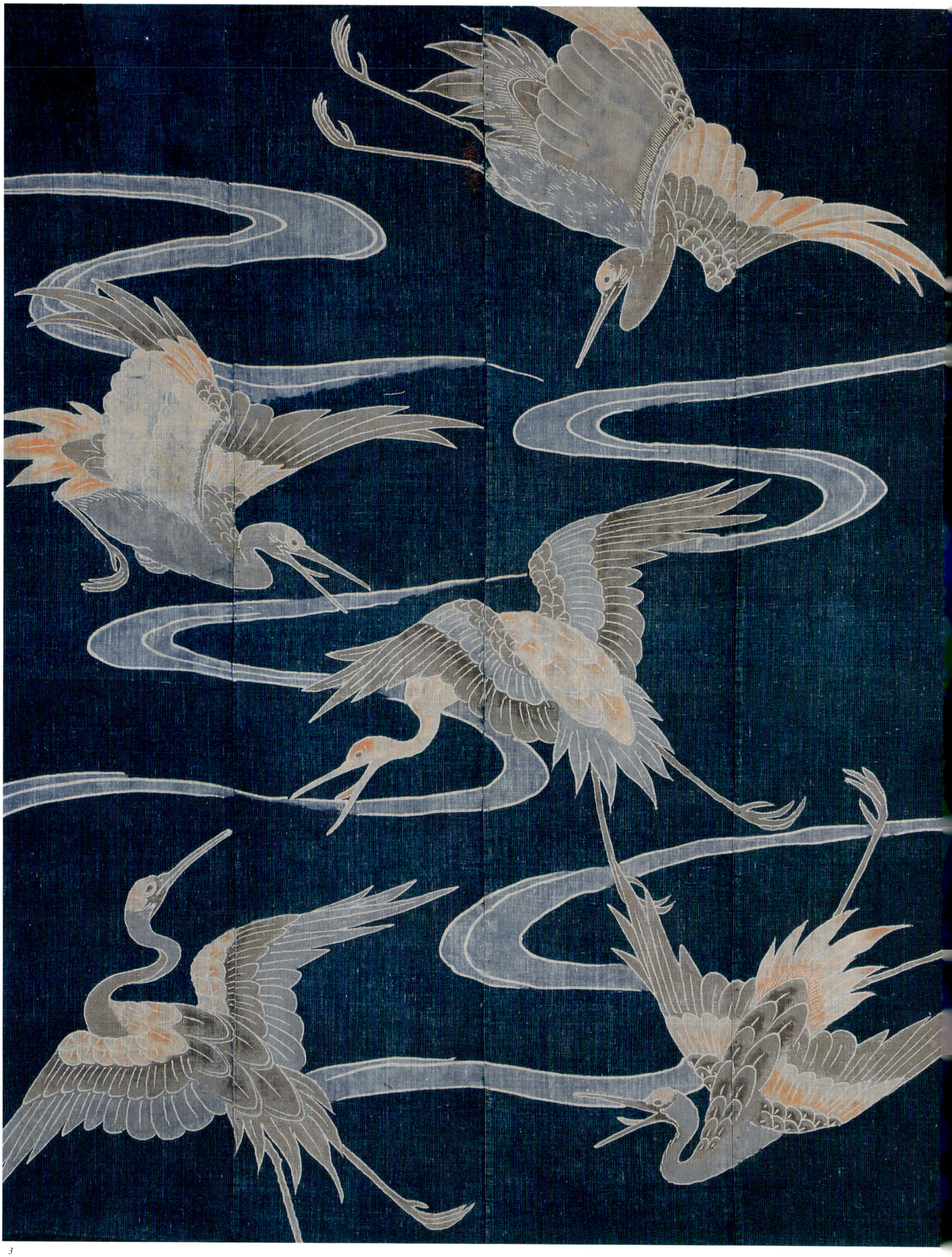

3

4

5

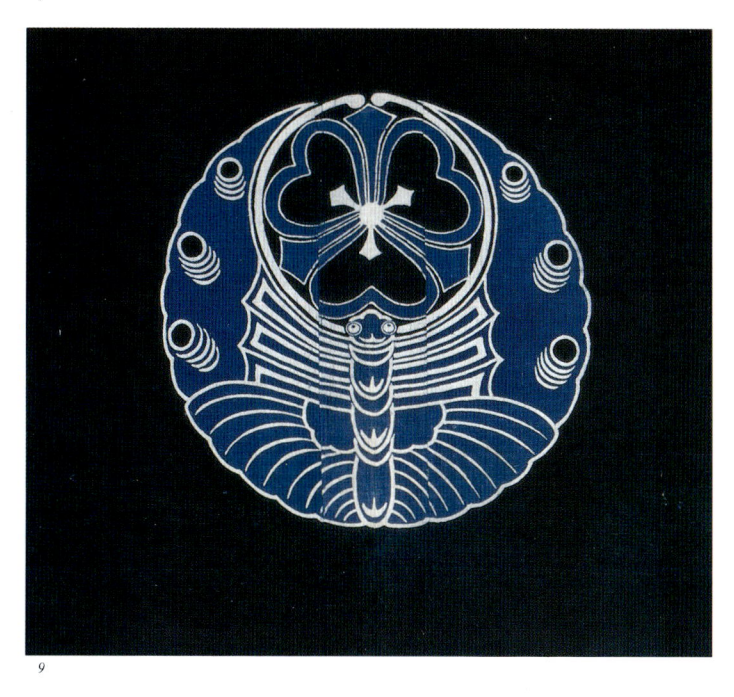

6

7

8

9

10

11

12

13

14

15

16

17

18

19

20

21

22

23

17

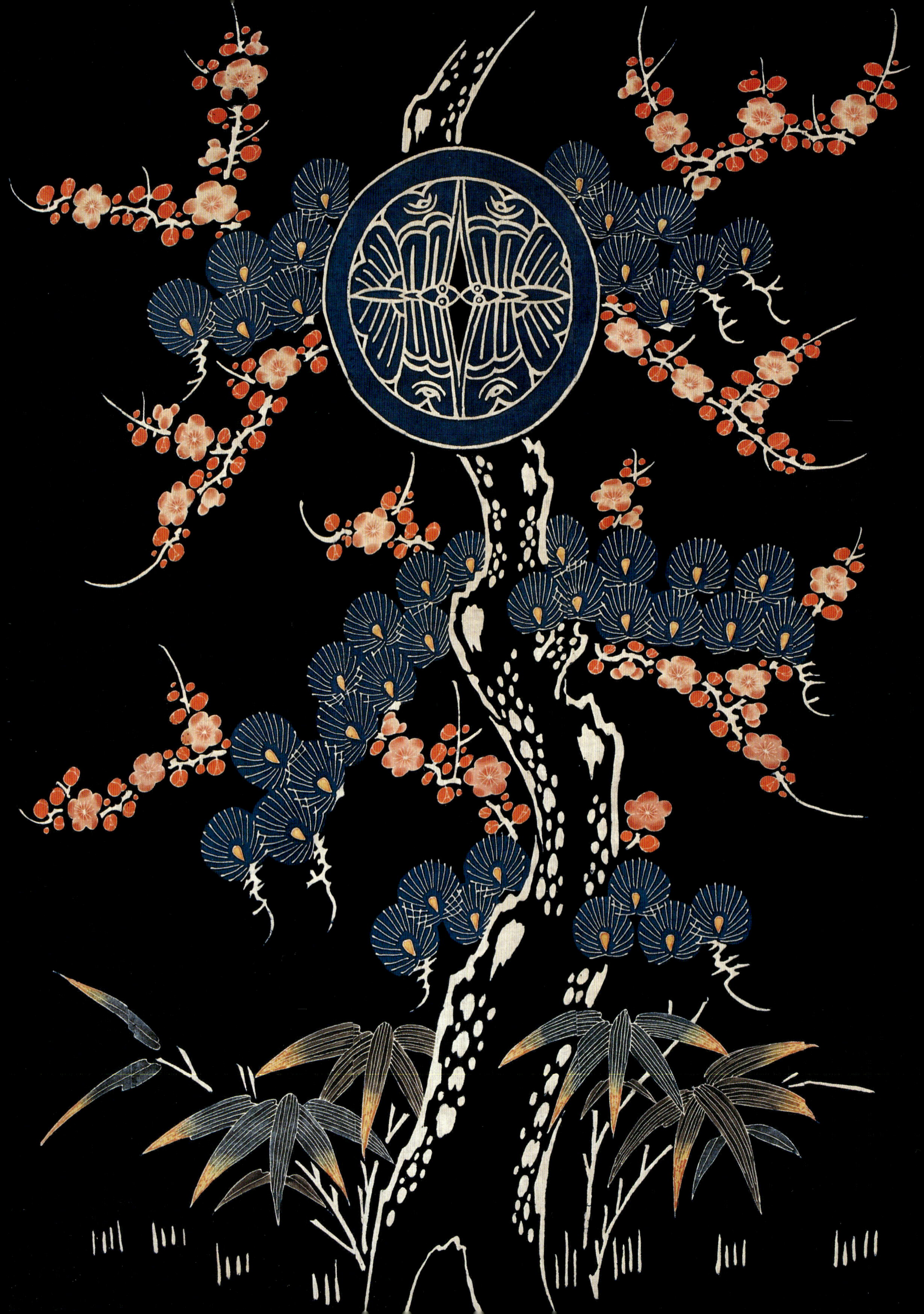

24

25

26

19

27

28

29

30

31

32

33

34

35

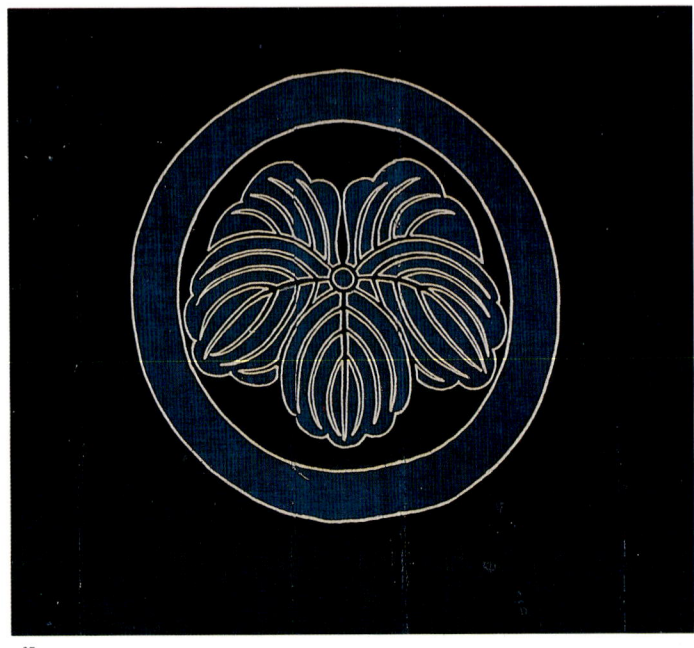

36 37

22

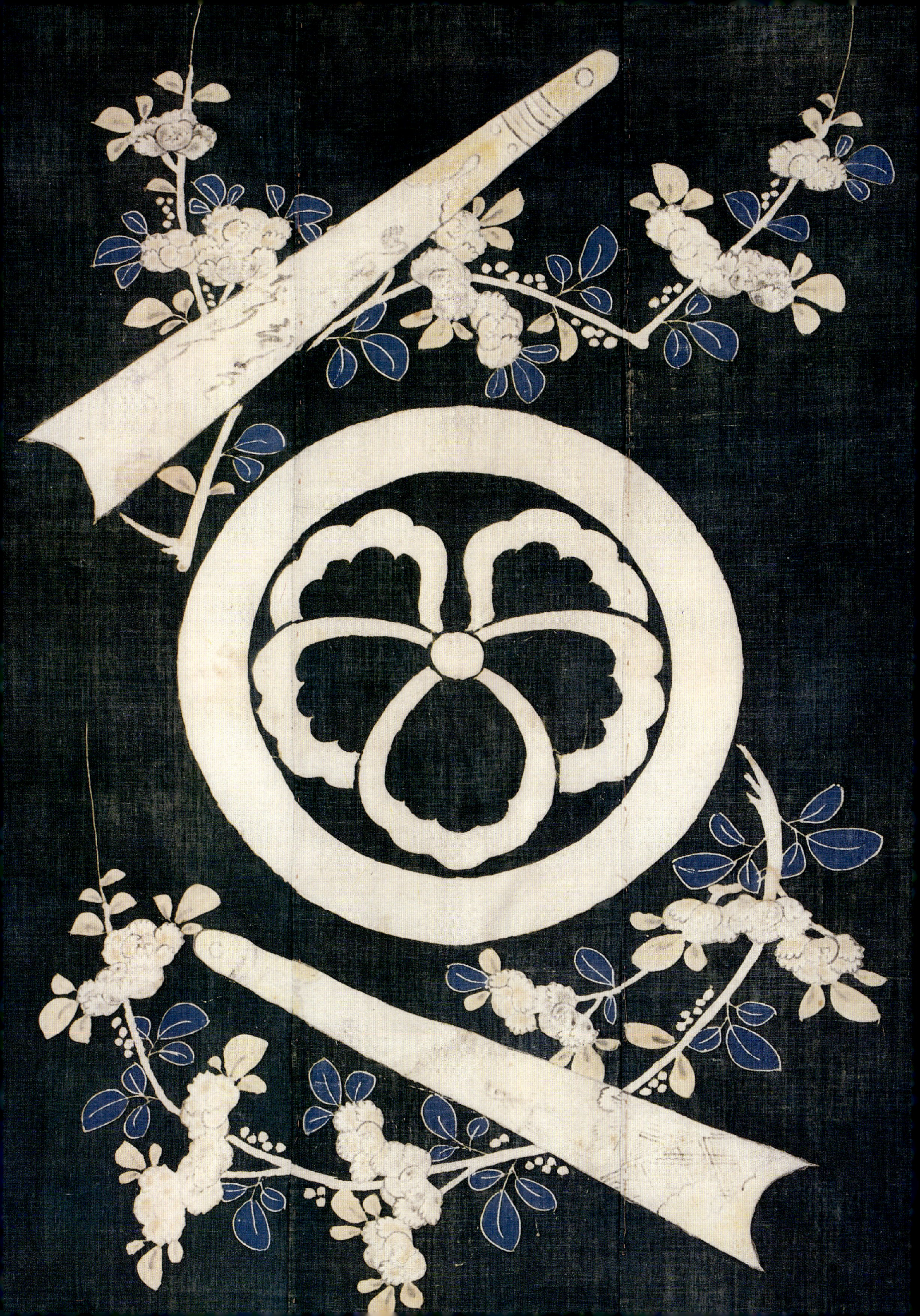

39

40

42

41

43

44

45

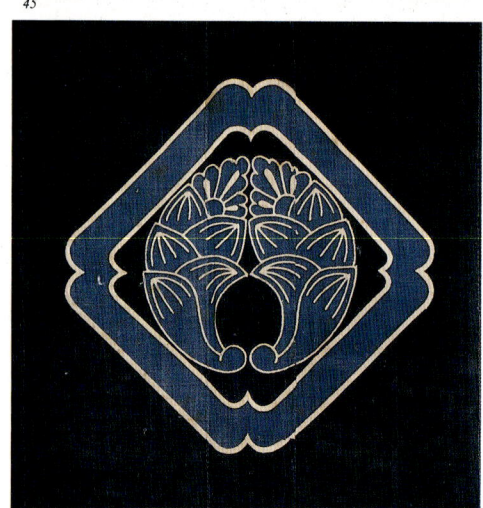

46

26

47

48

50

49

51

52

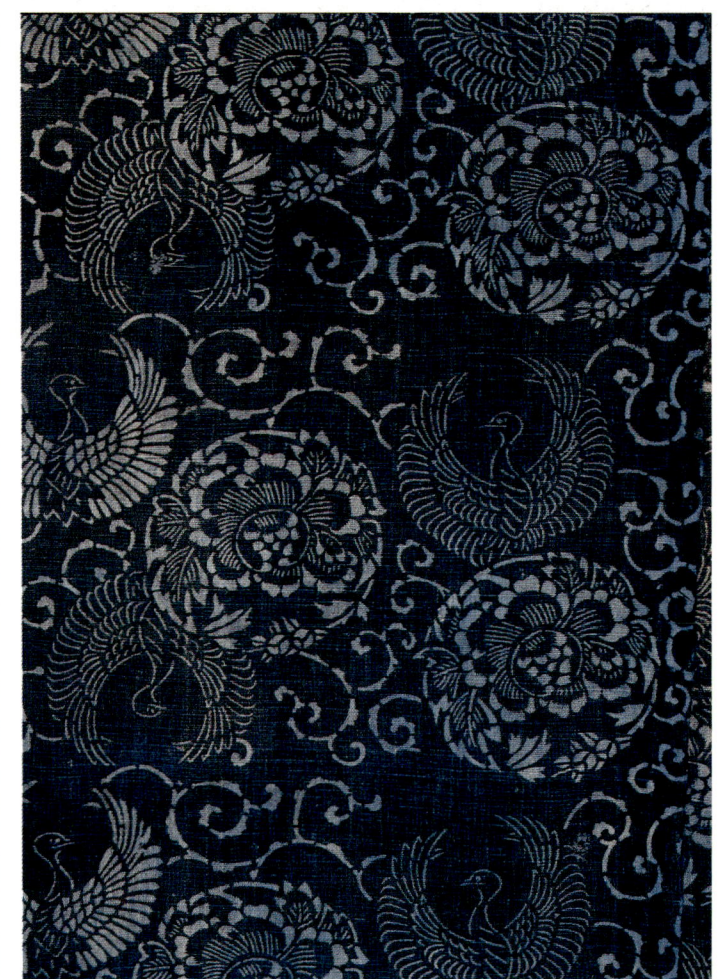

53

54

55

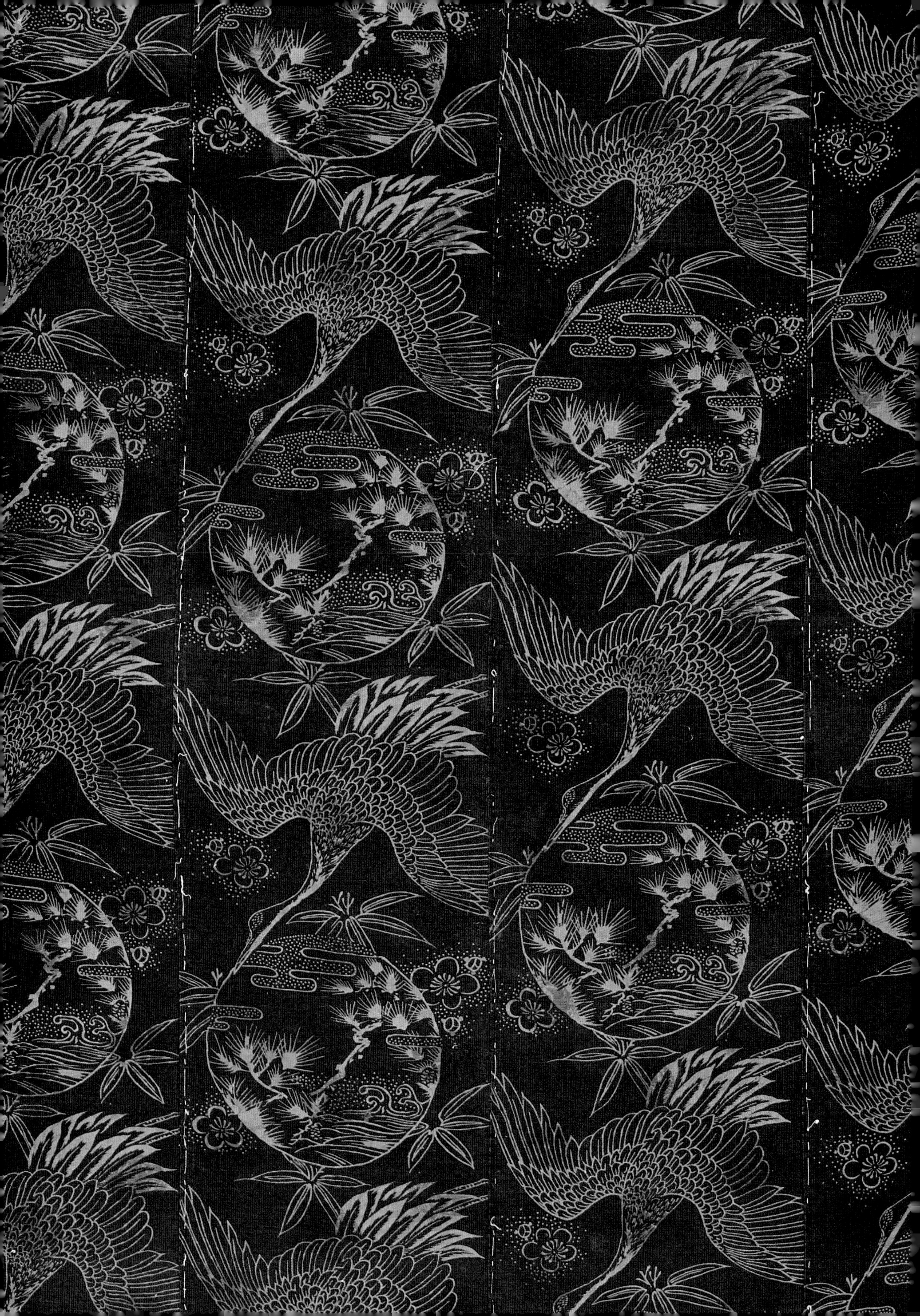

57

58

59

60

61

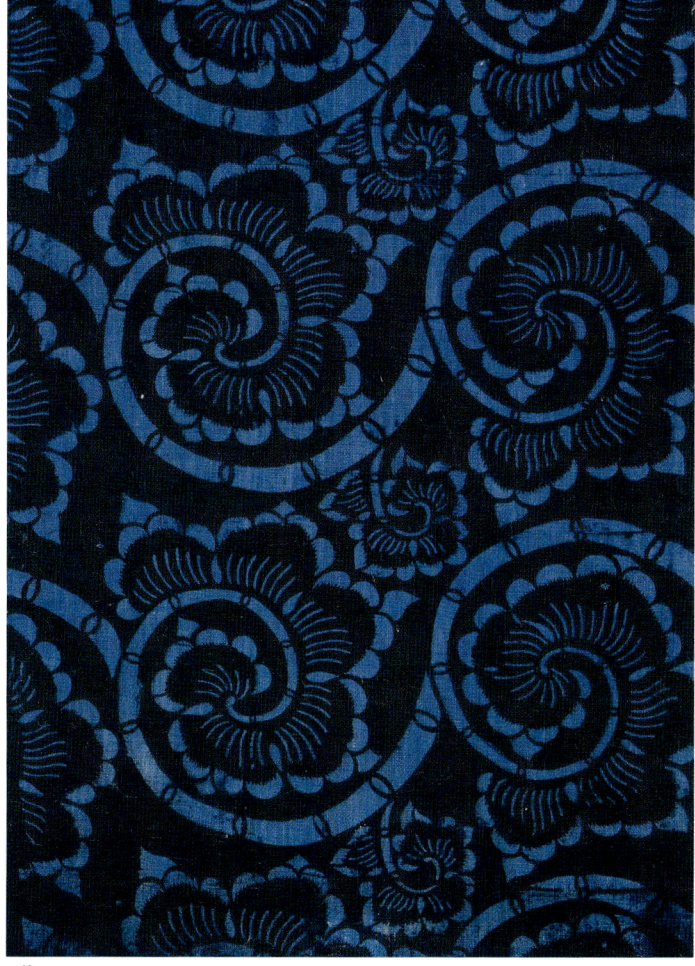

62

63

64

SHIMA;Stripes

縞

65

66

67

68

69

70

71

72

73

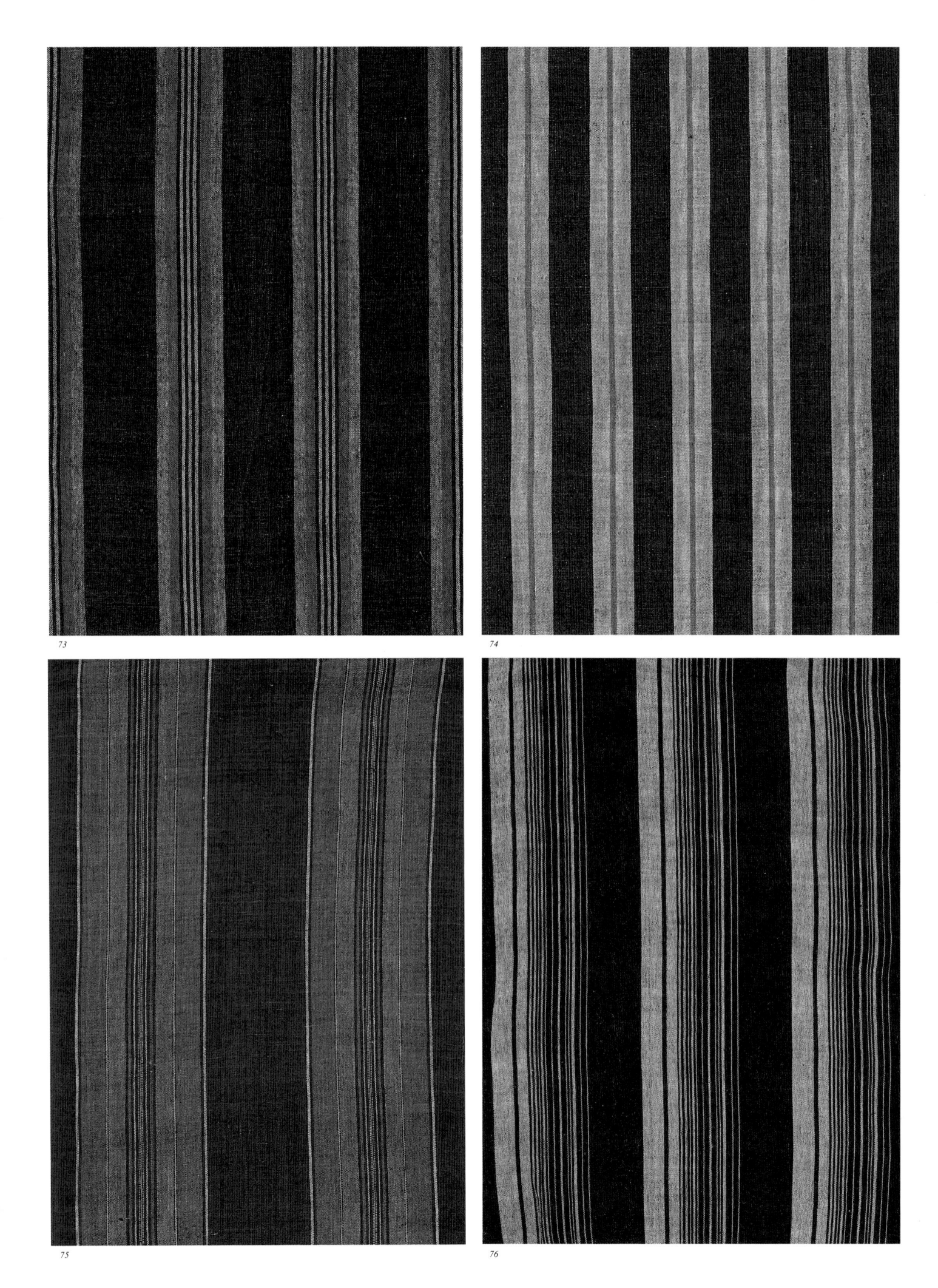

74

75

76

77

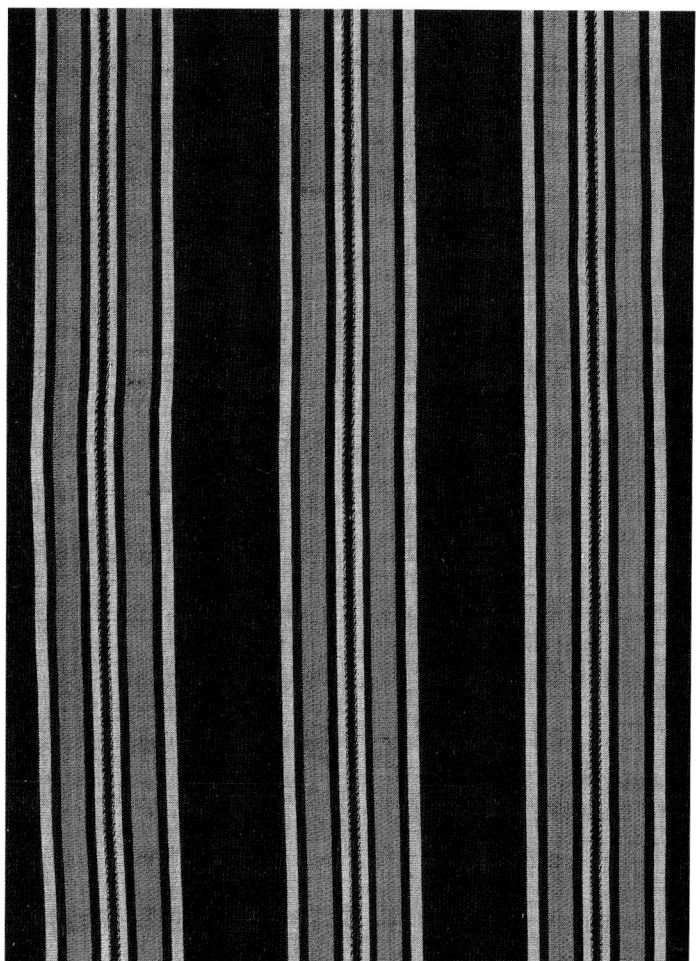

78

79

80

KŌSHI; Lattice

格子

81

82

83

84

85

86

87

88

89

90

91

92

93

41

94

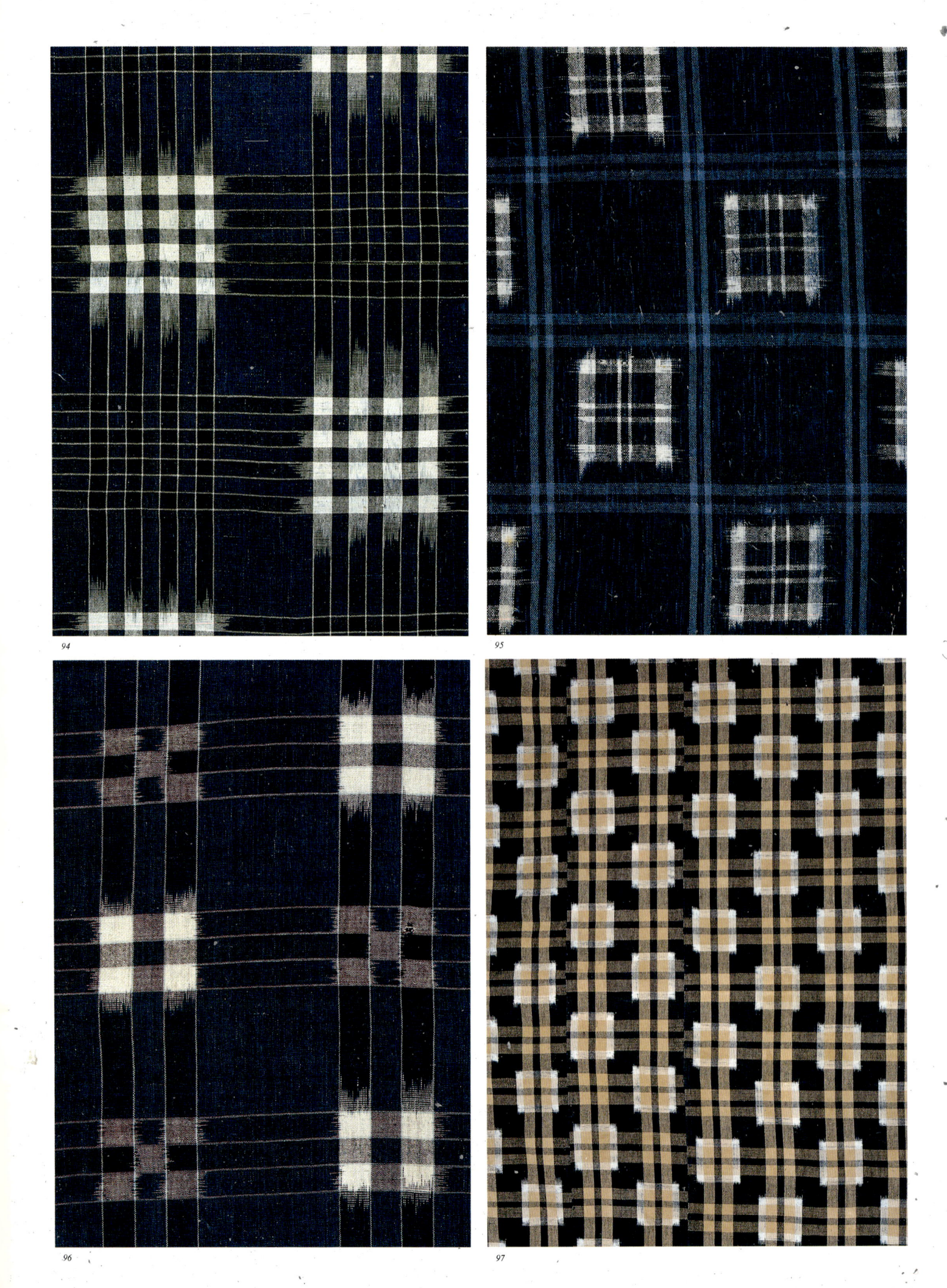

95

96

97

98

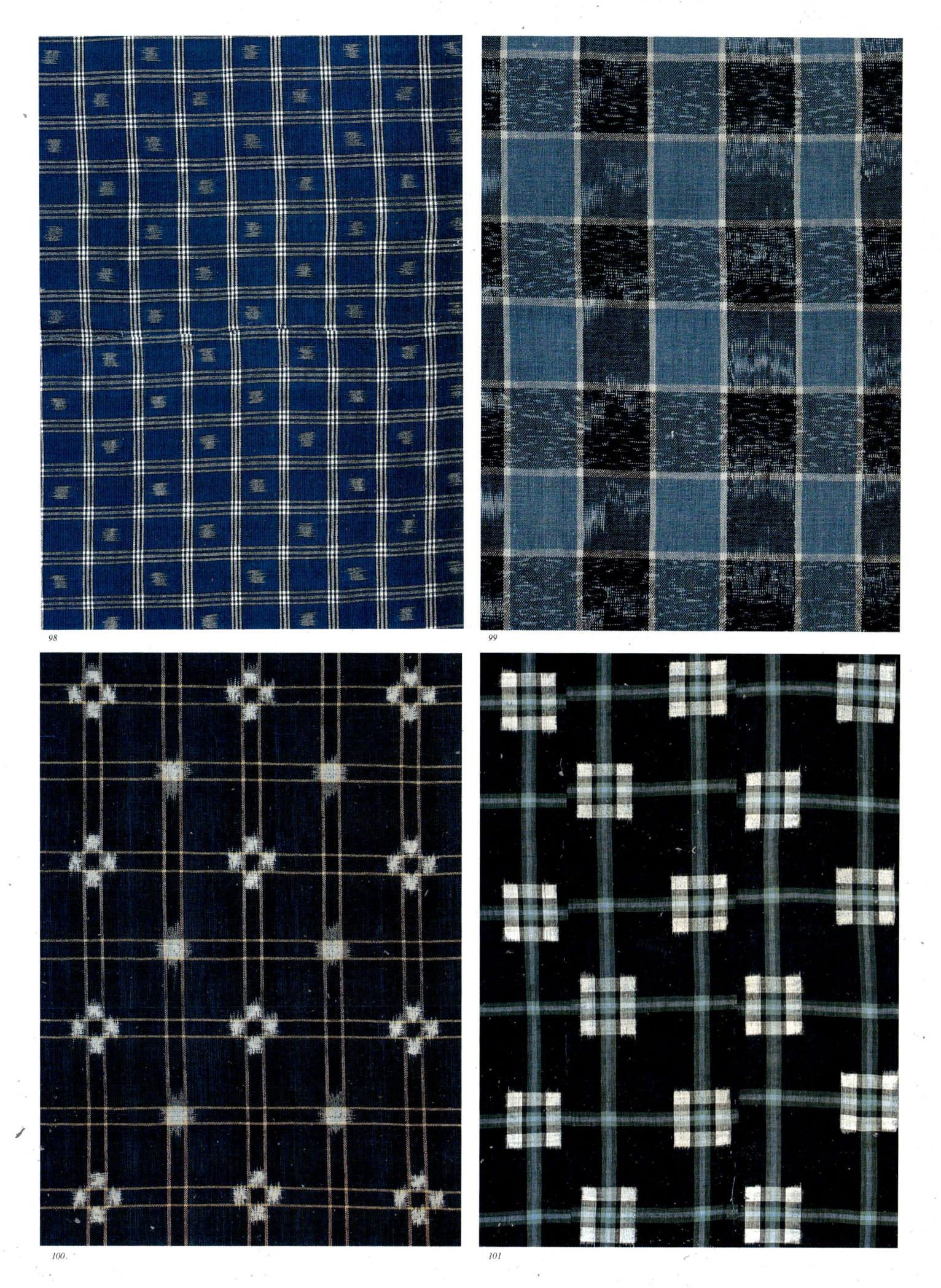

99

100

101

KASURI:*Ikat*

絣

103

104

105

106

45

107

108

109

110

111

112

113

114

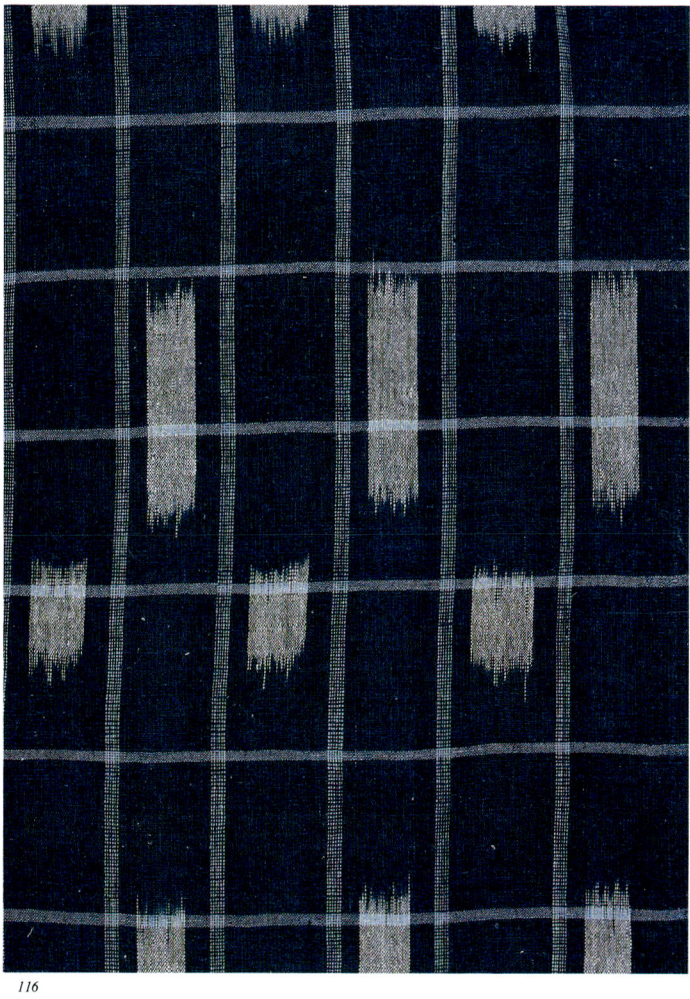

115

116

117

118

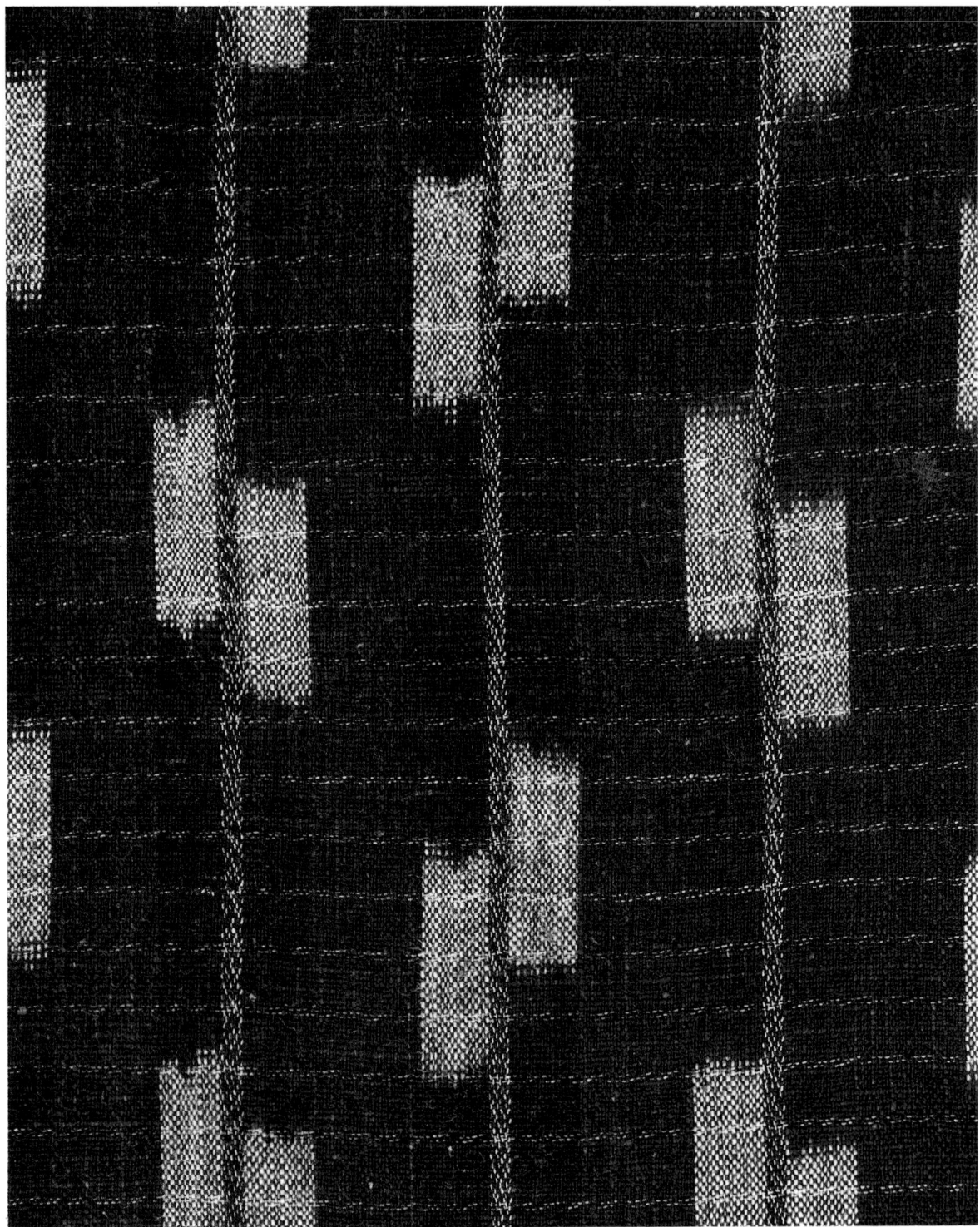

119

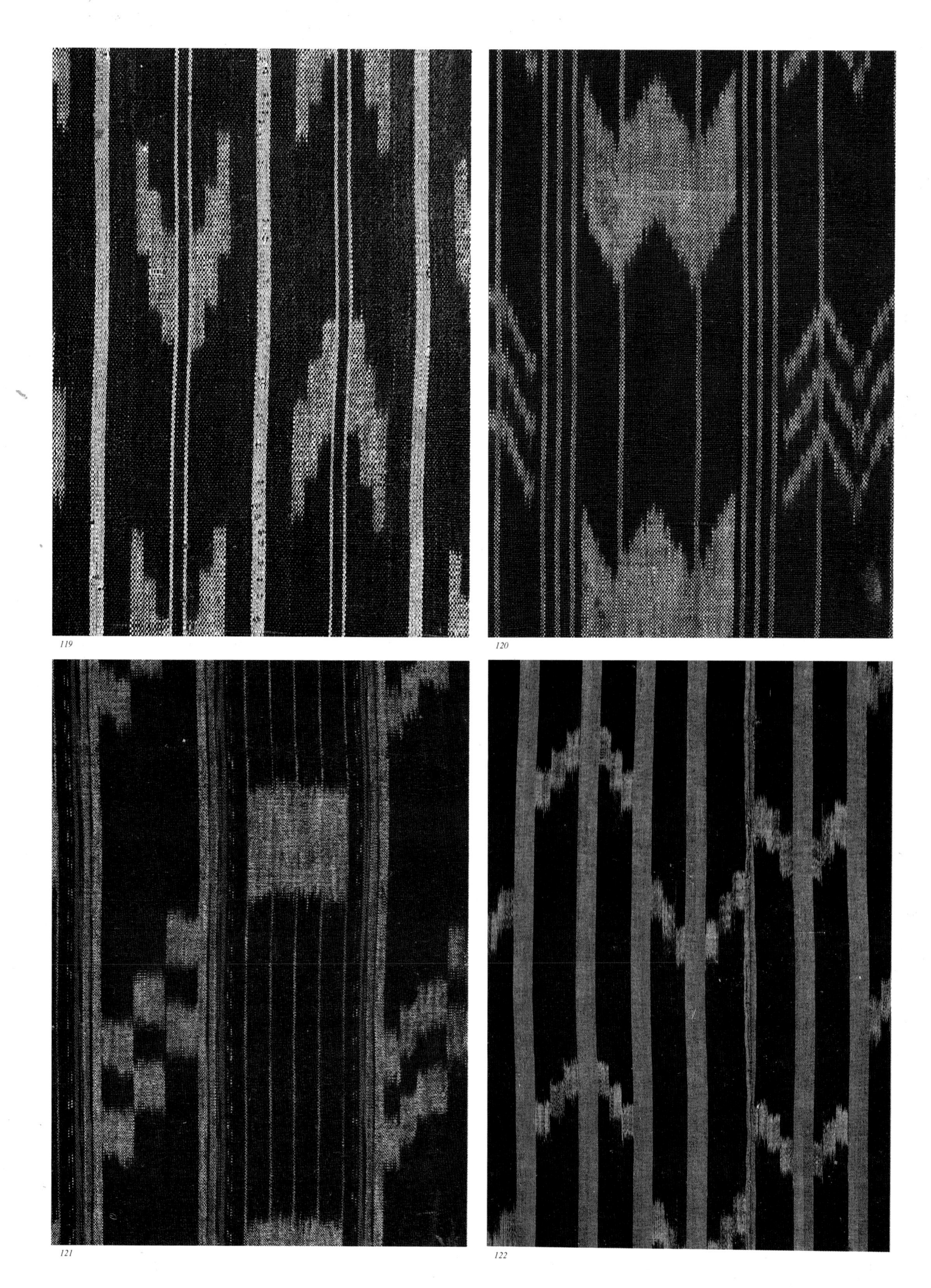

120

121

122

絵画文様
Pictorial patterns

123

124

125

126

127

128

129

130

131

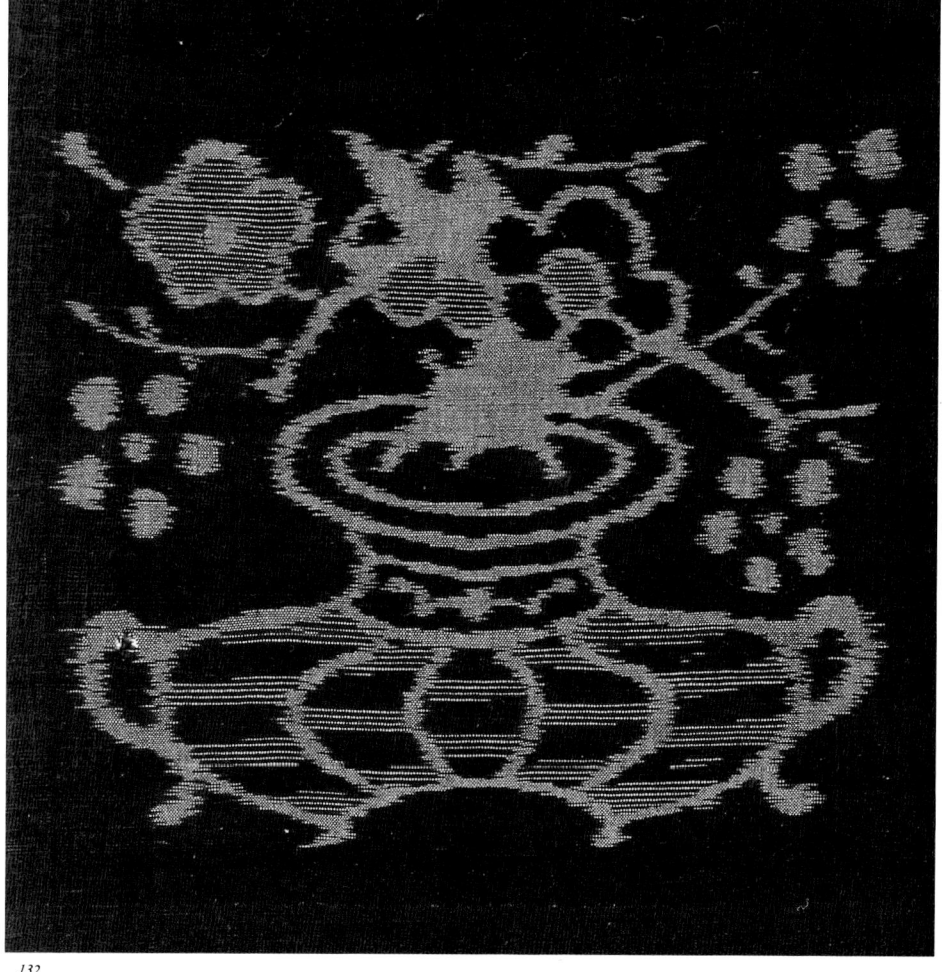

132

133

134

135

136

137

59

138

139

140

141

142

143

144

145

146

147

148

149

150

151

152

153

154

155

156

157

158

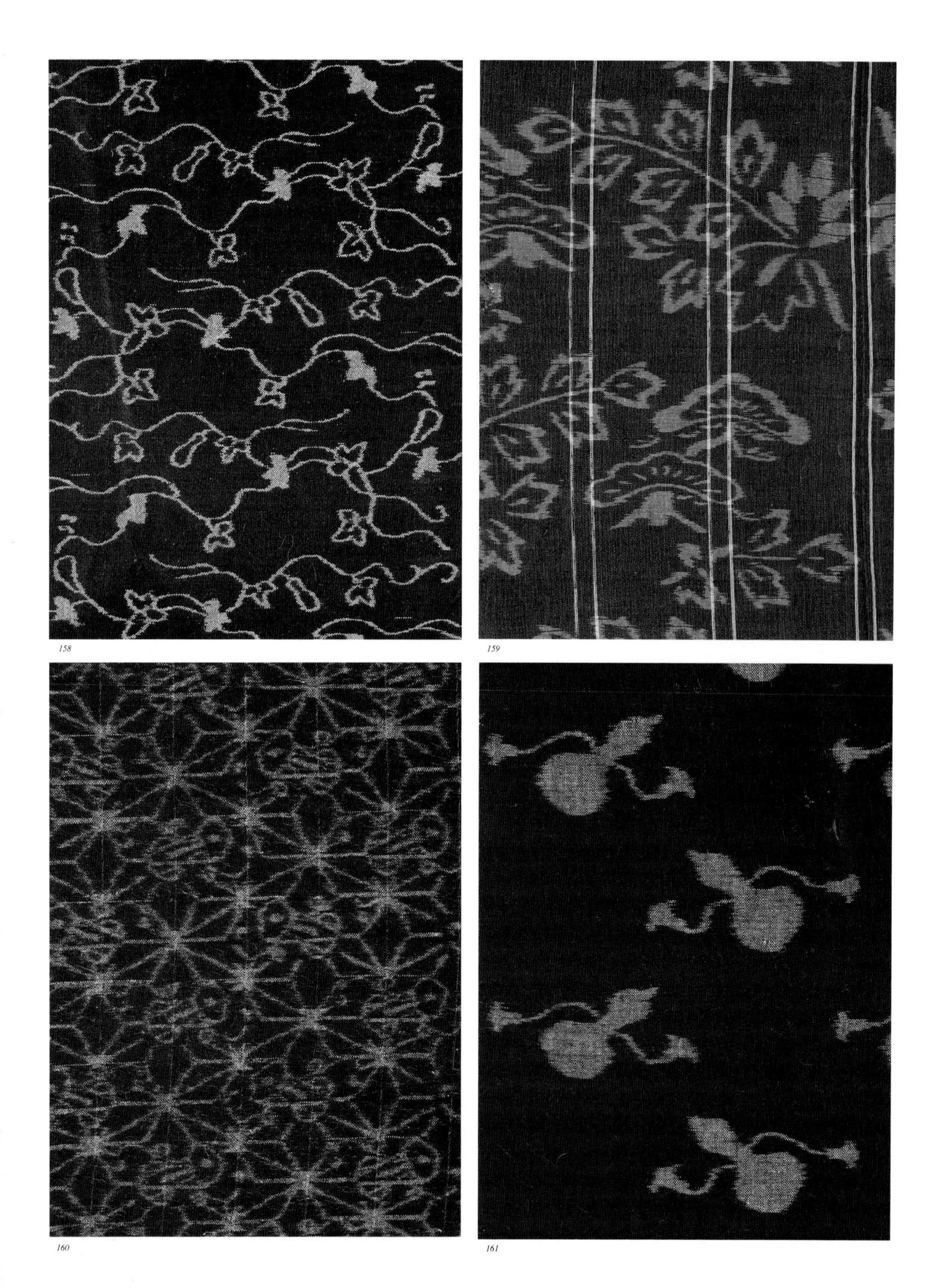

159

160

161

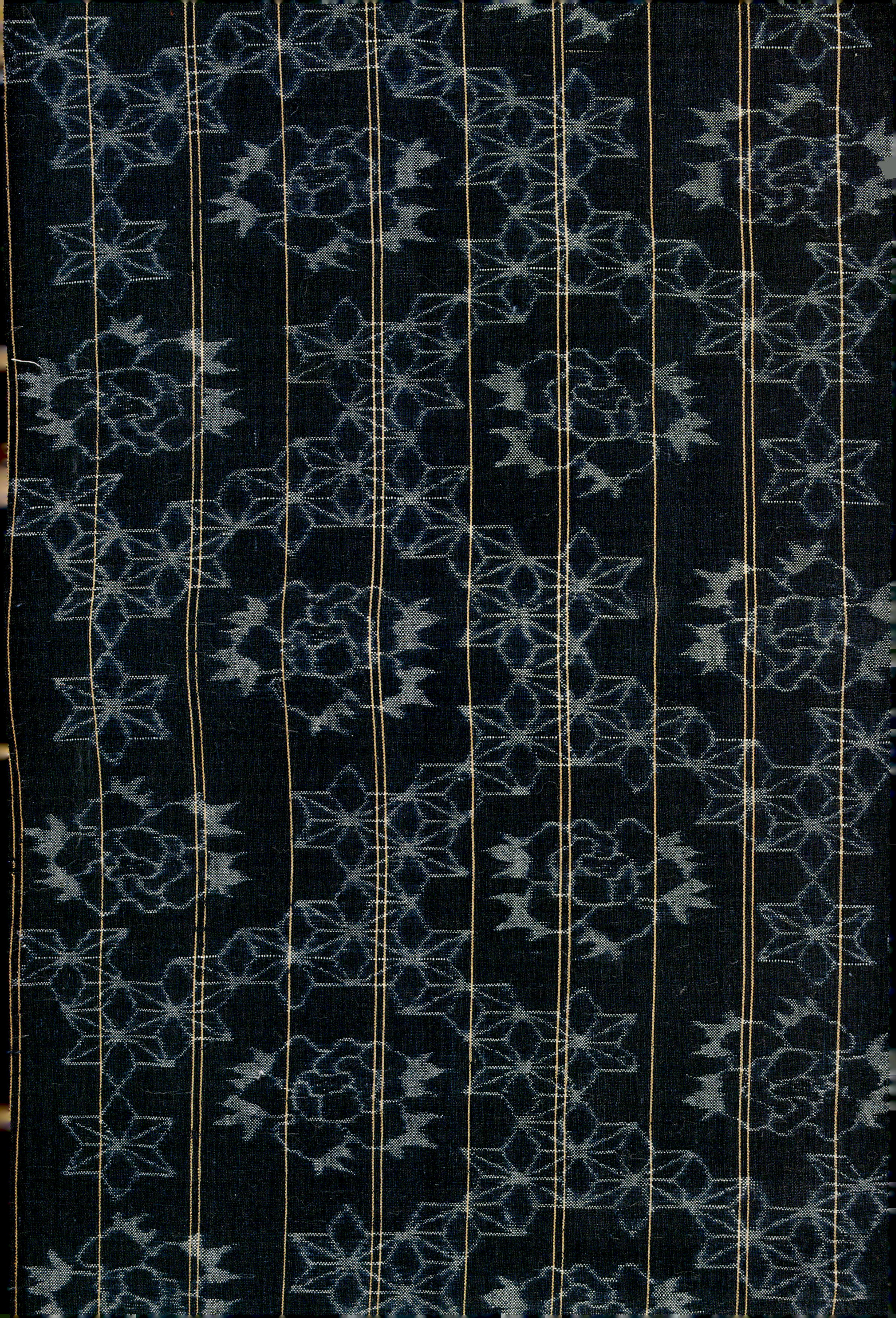

163

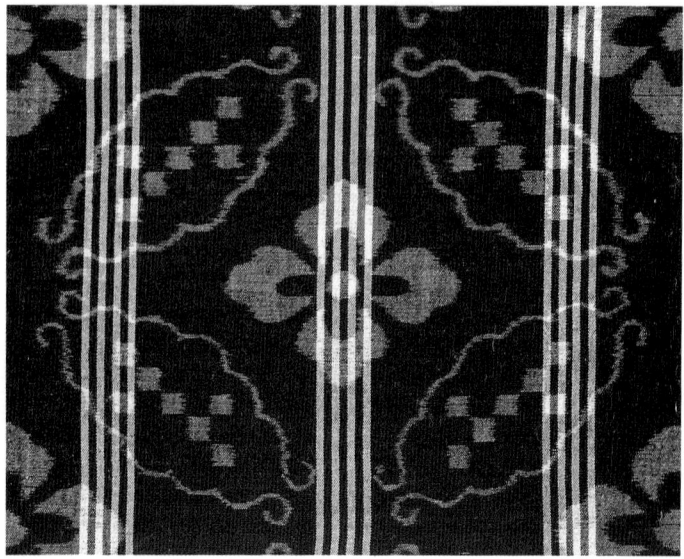

164

165

166

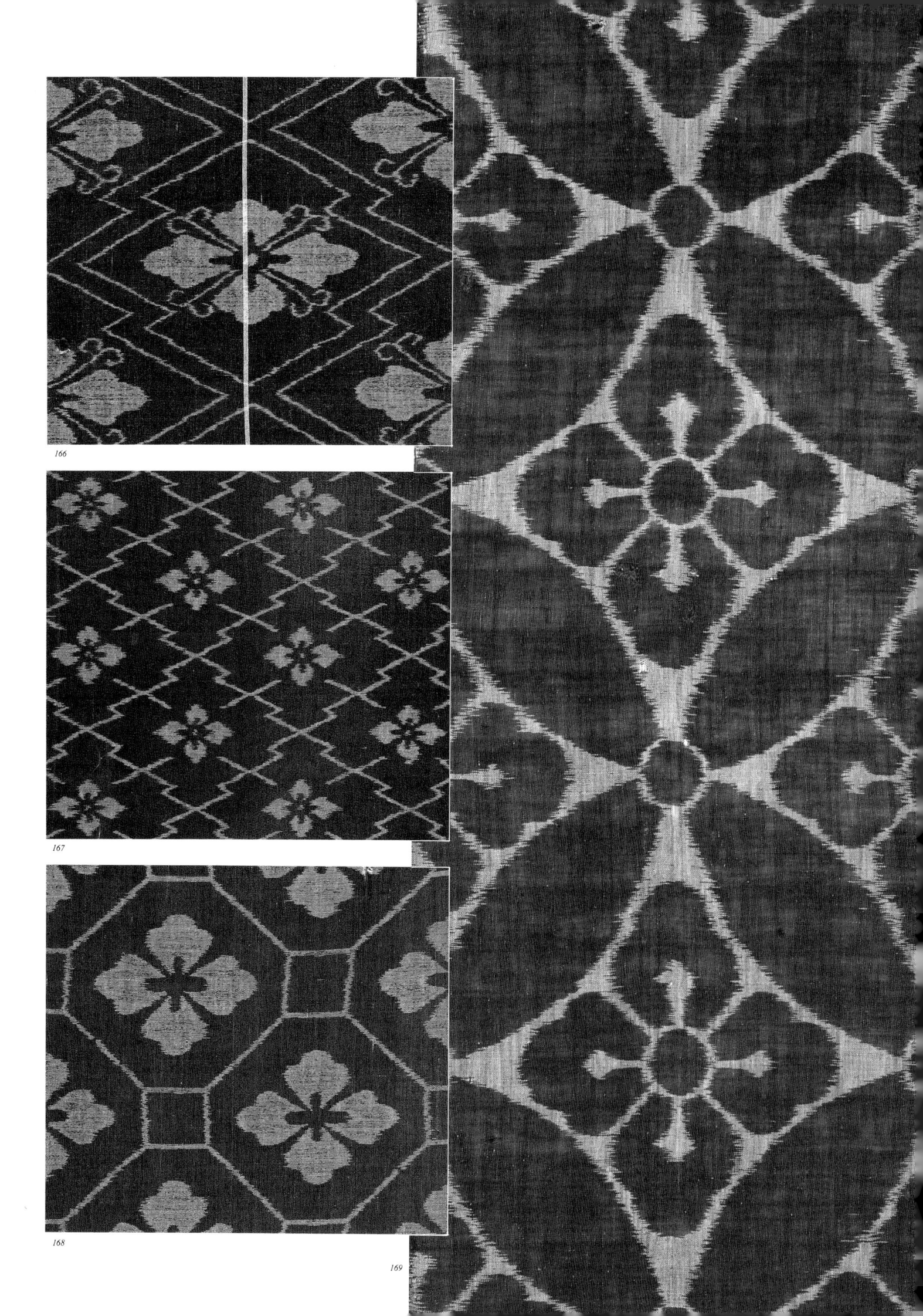

167

168

169

170

171

172

173

70

174

175

176

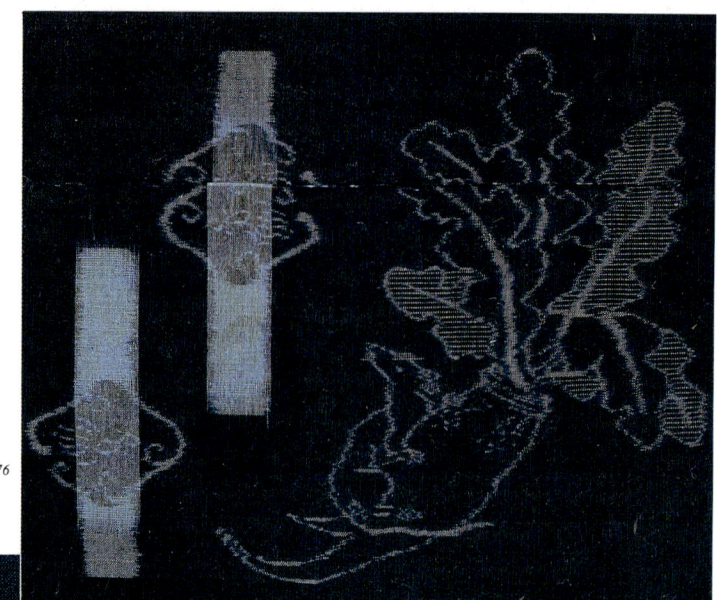

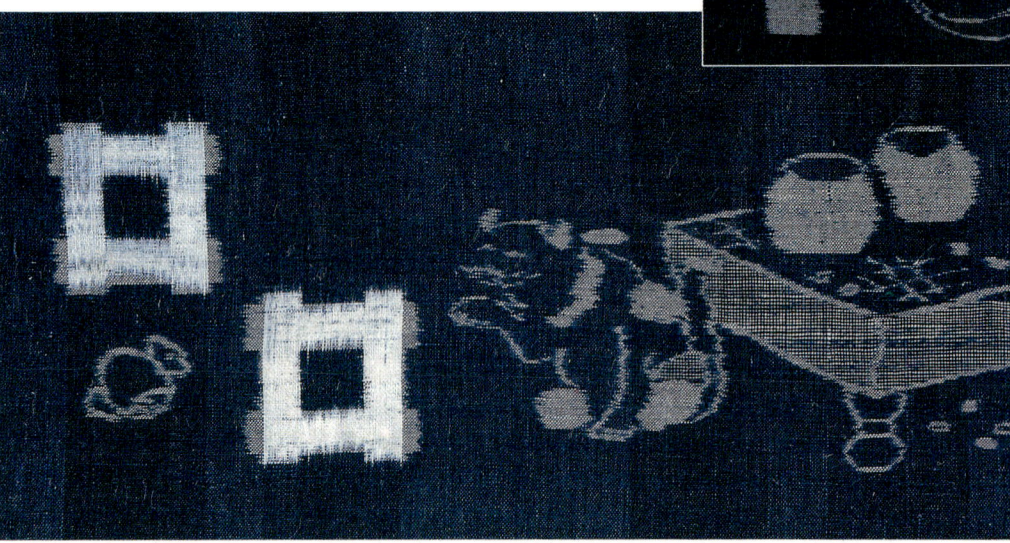

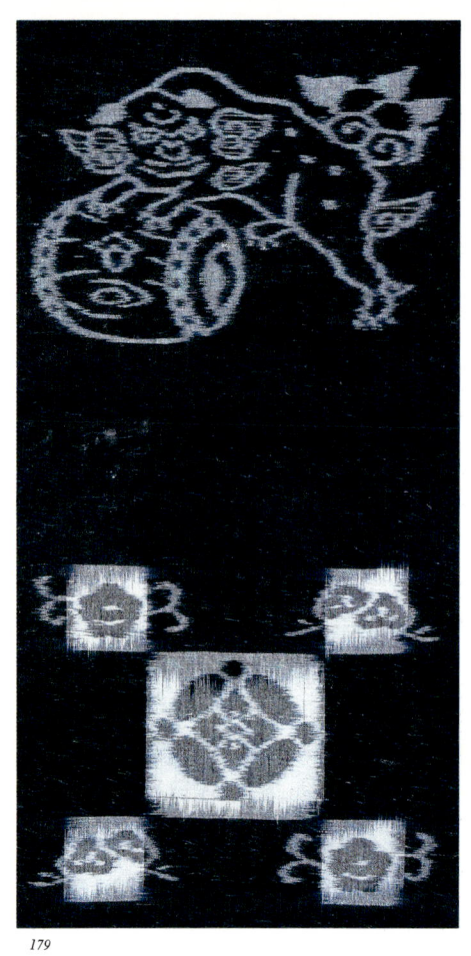

177

178

179

180

181

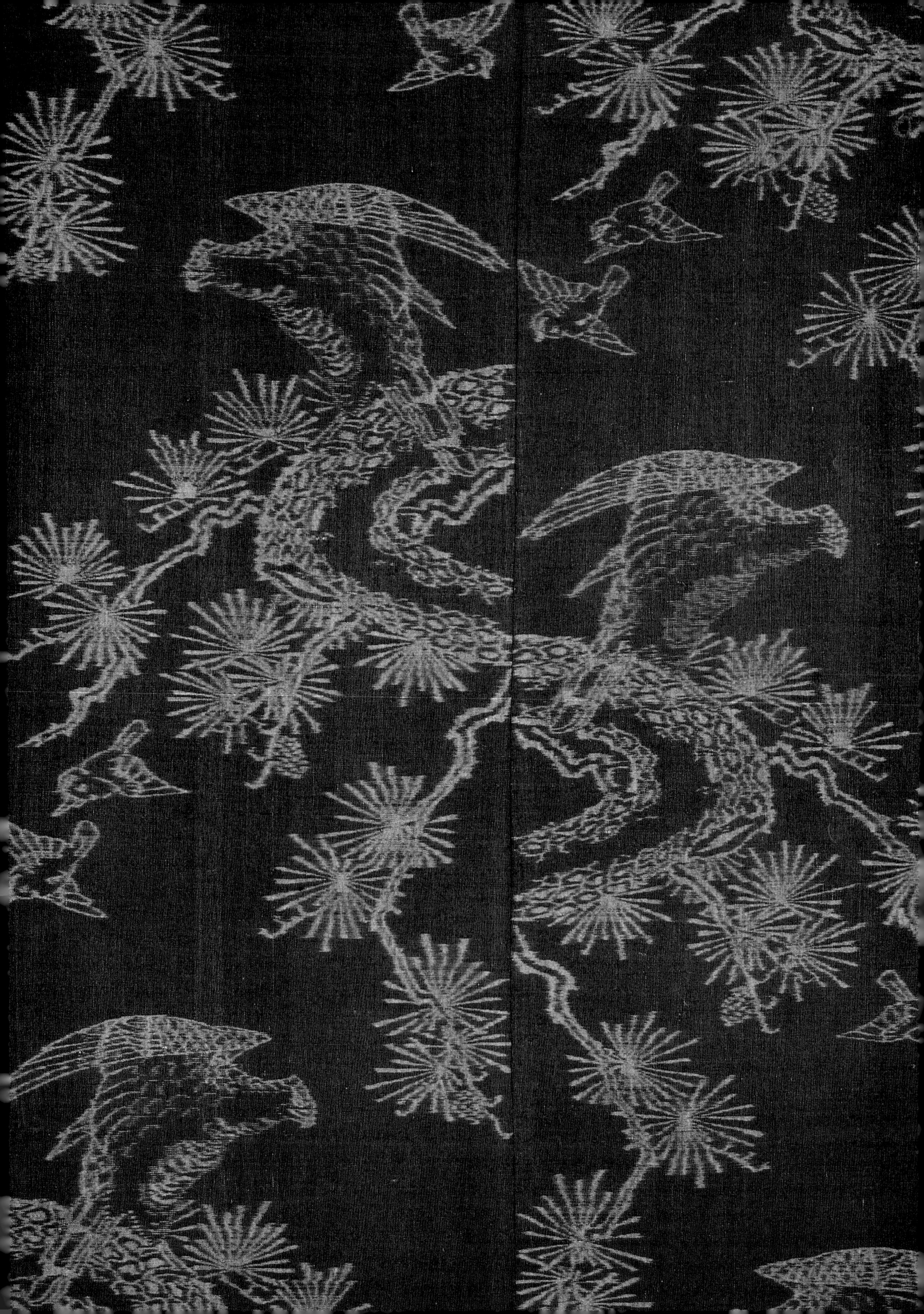

183

184

185

186

75

187

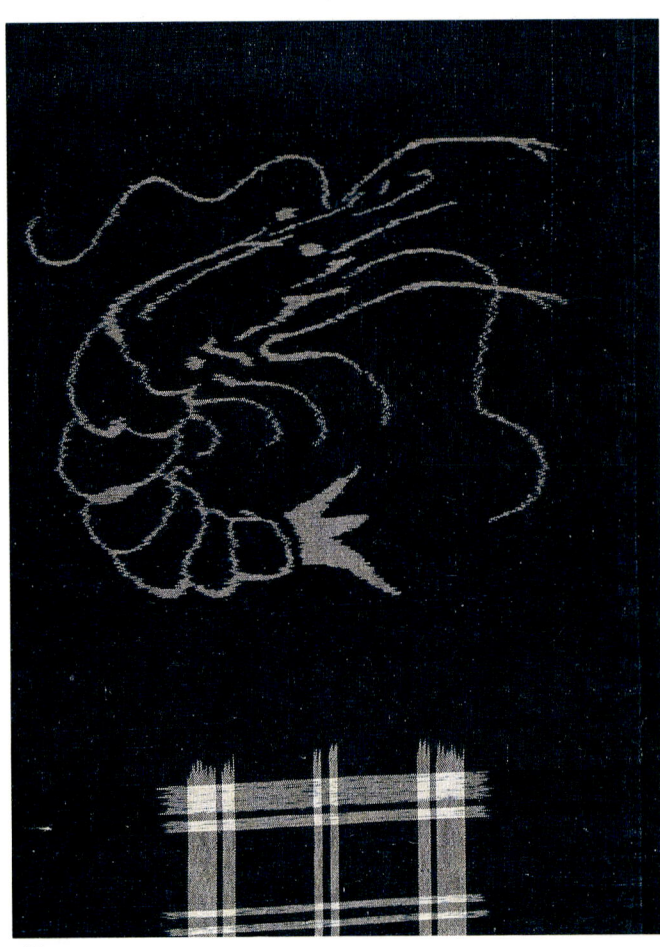

188

189

190

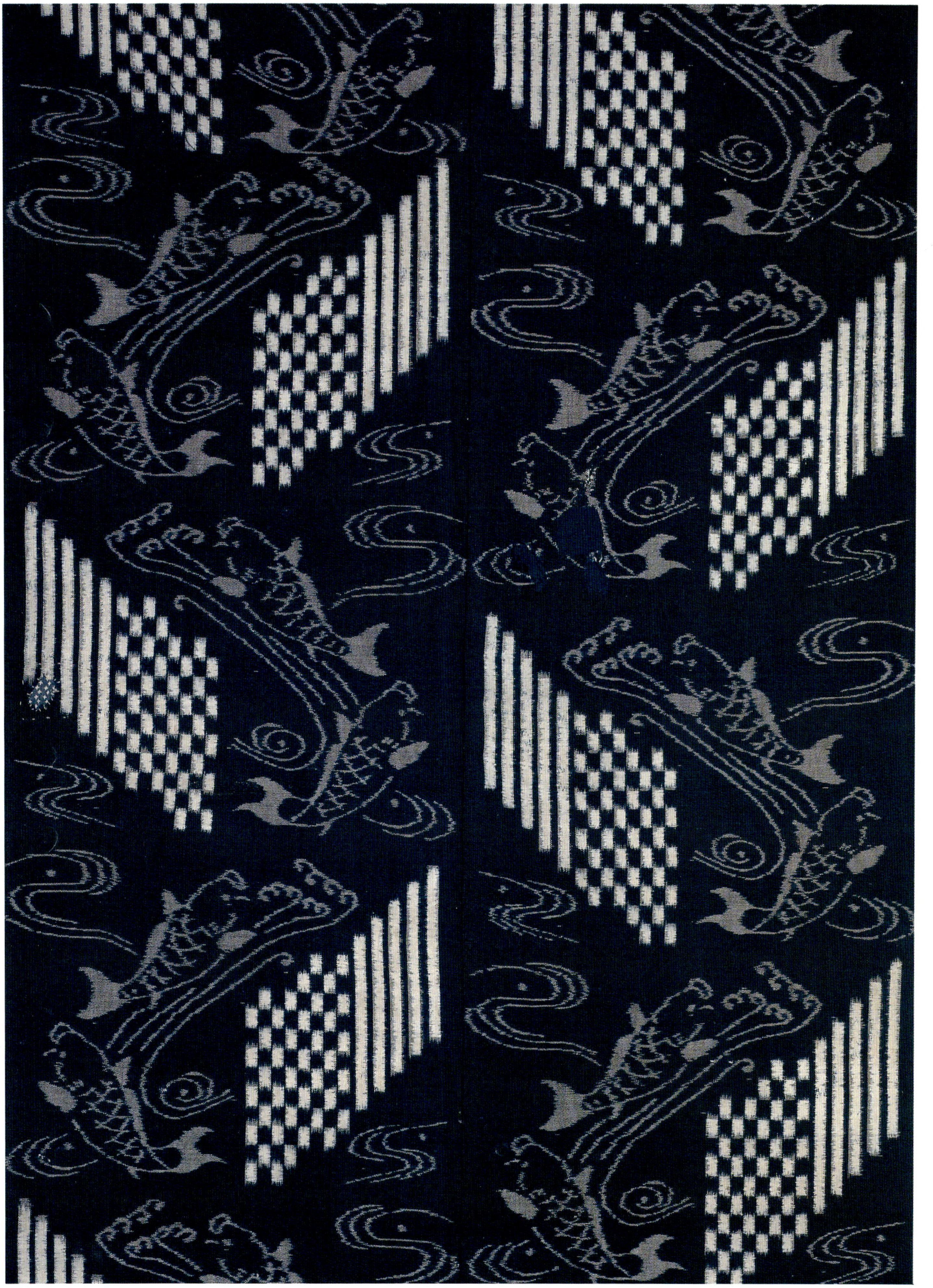
191

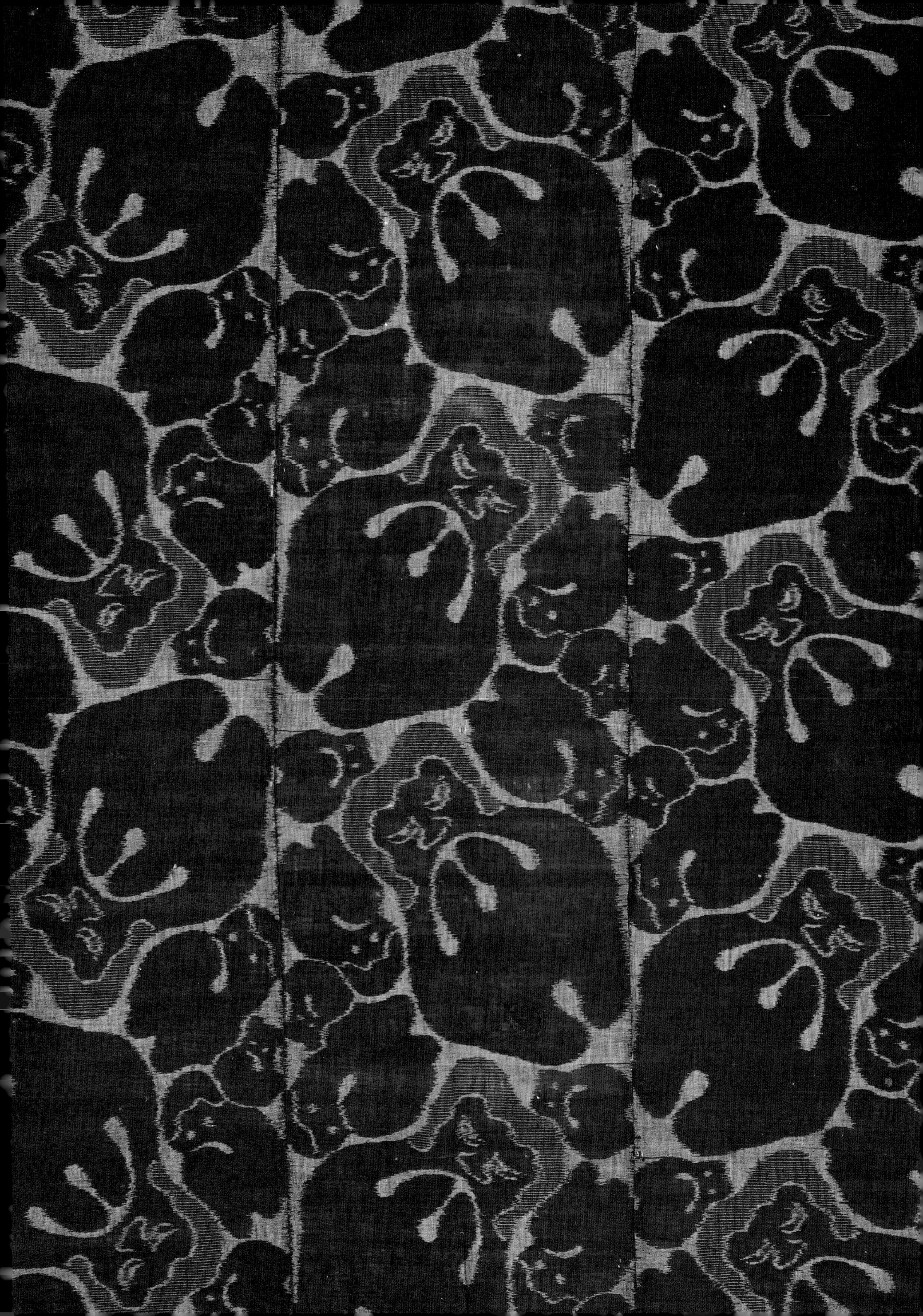

193

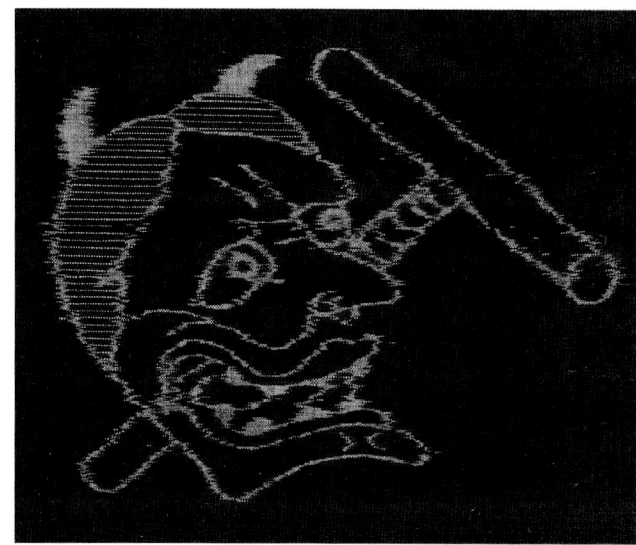

194

195

196

197

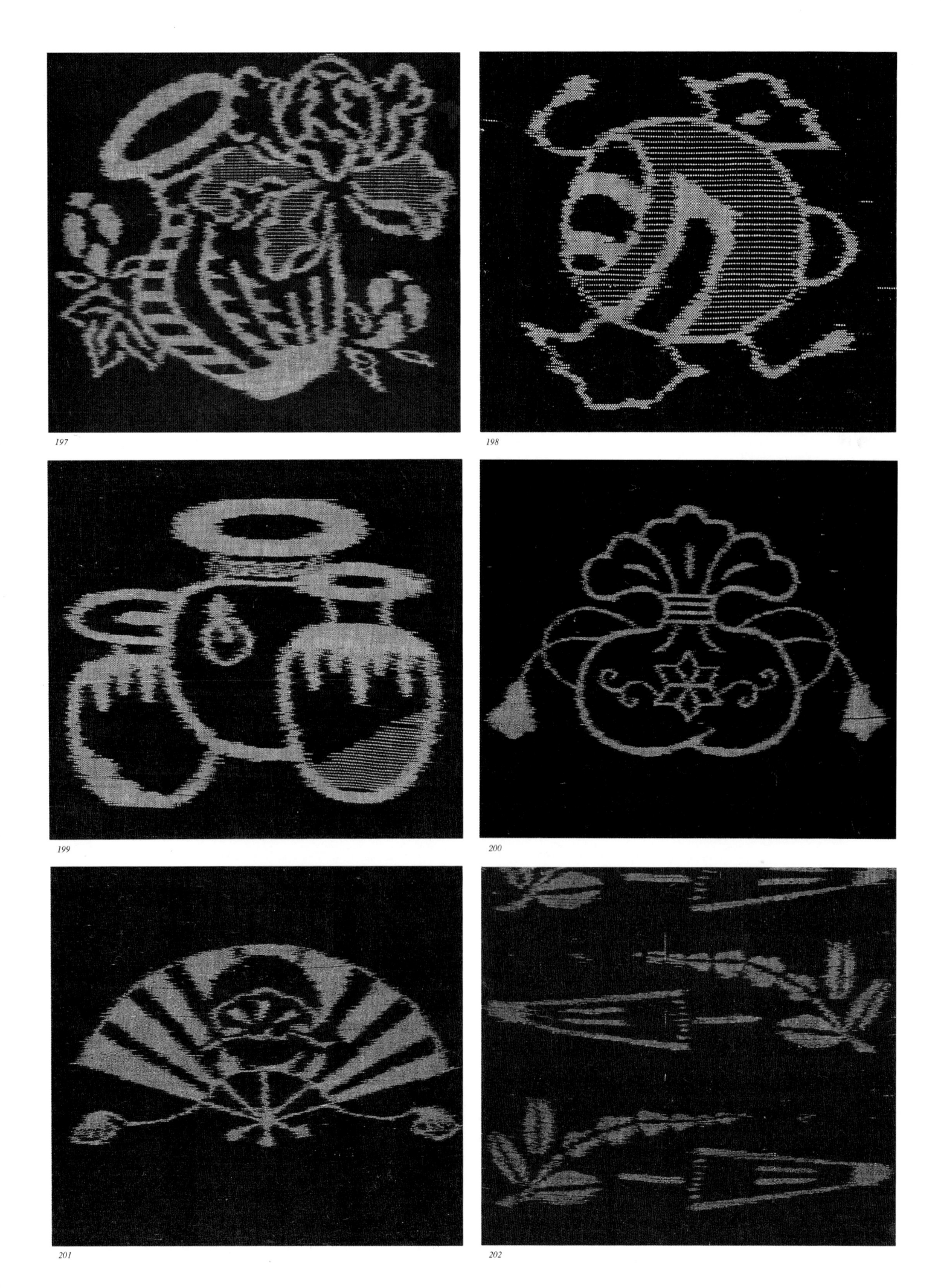

198

199

200

201

202

80

203

204

205

206

81

207

208

209

210

211

212

213

幾何文様
― Geometric patterns ―

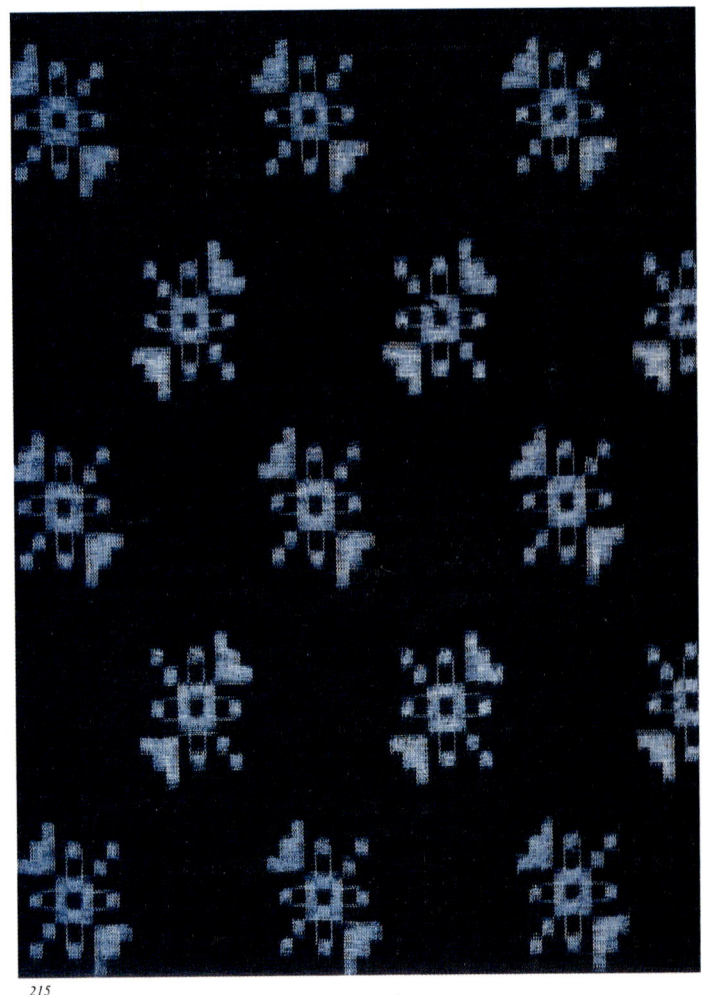

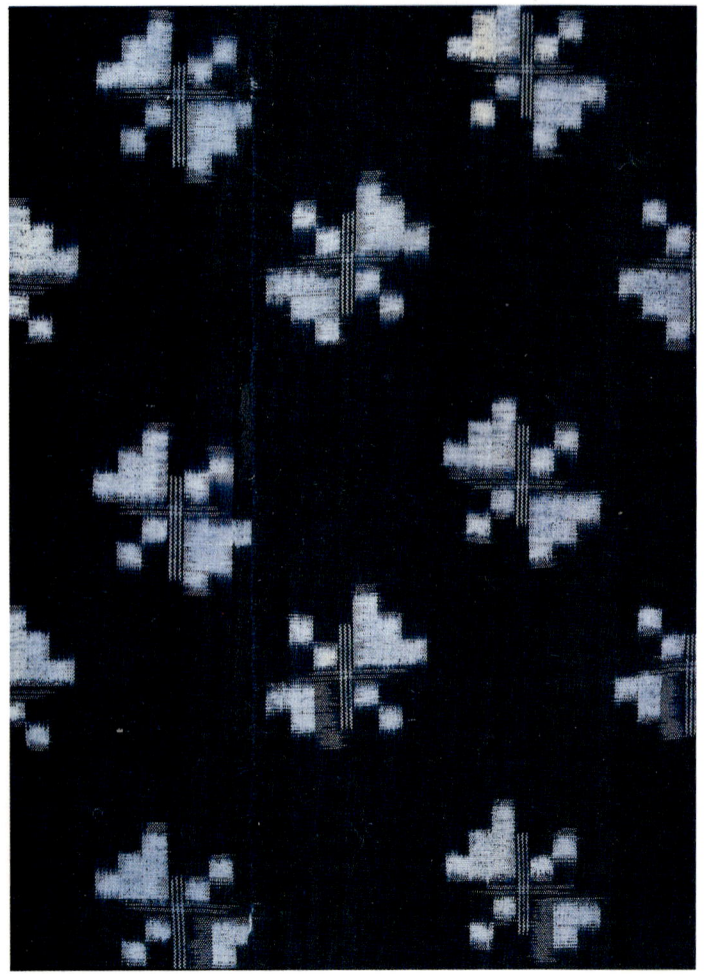

214

215

216

217

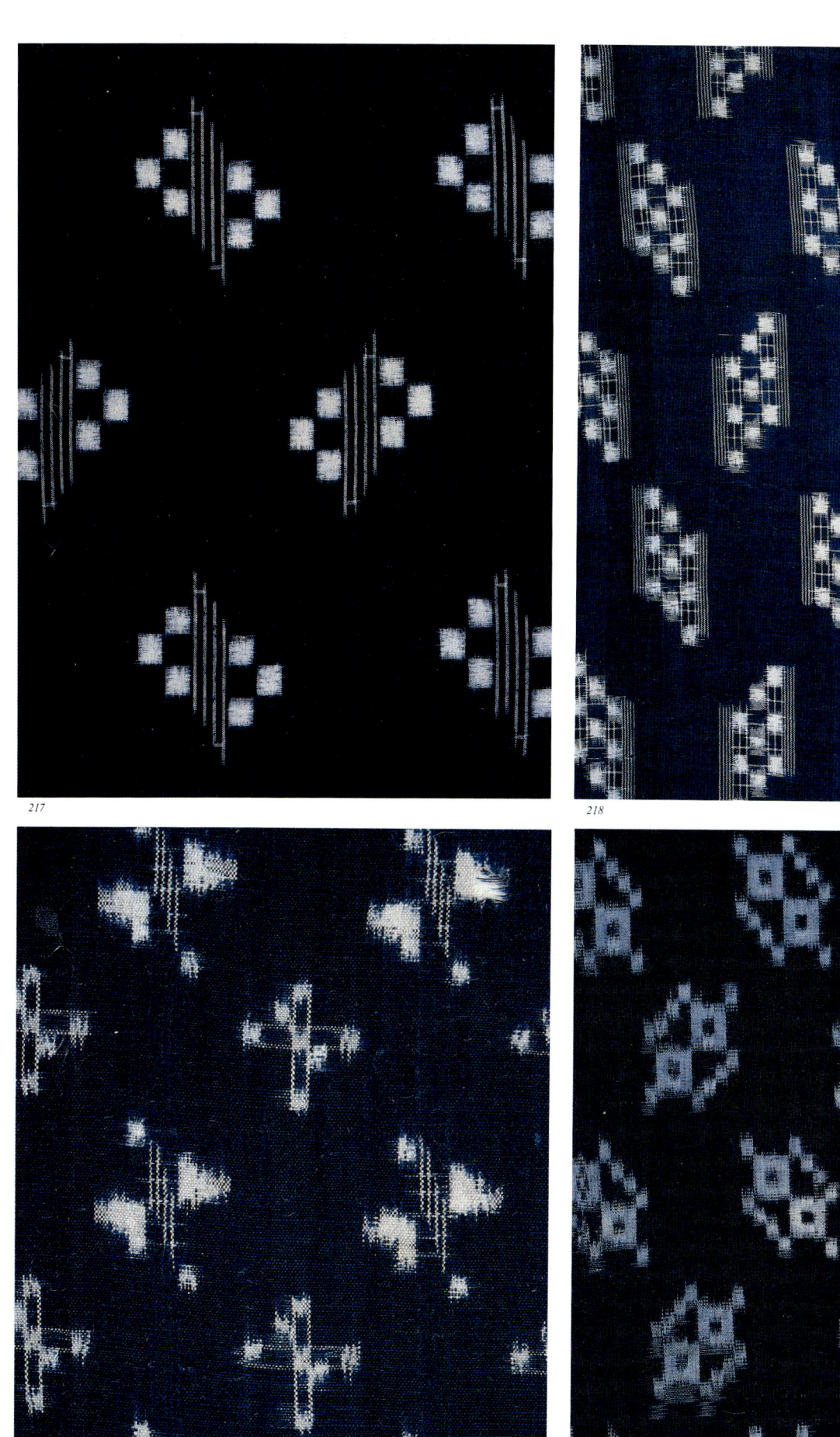

218

219

220

85

221

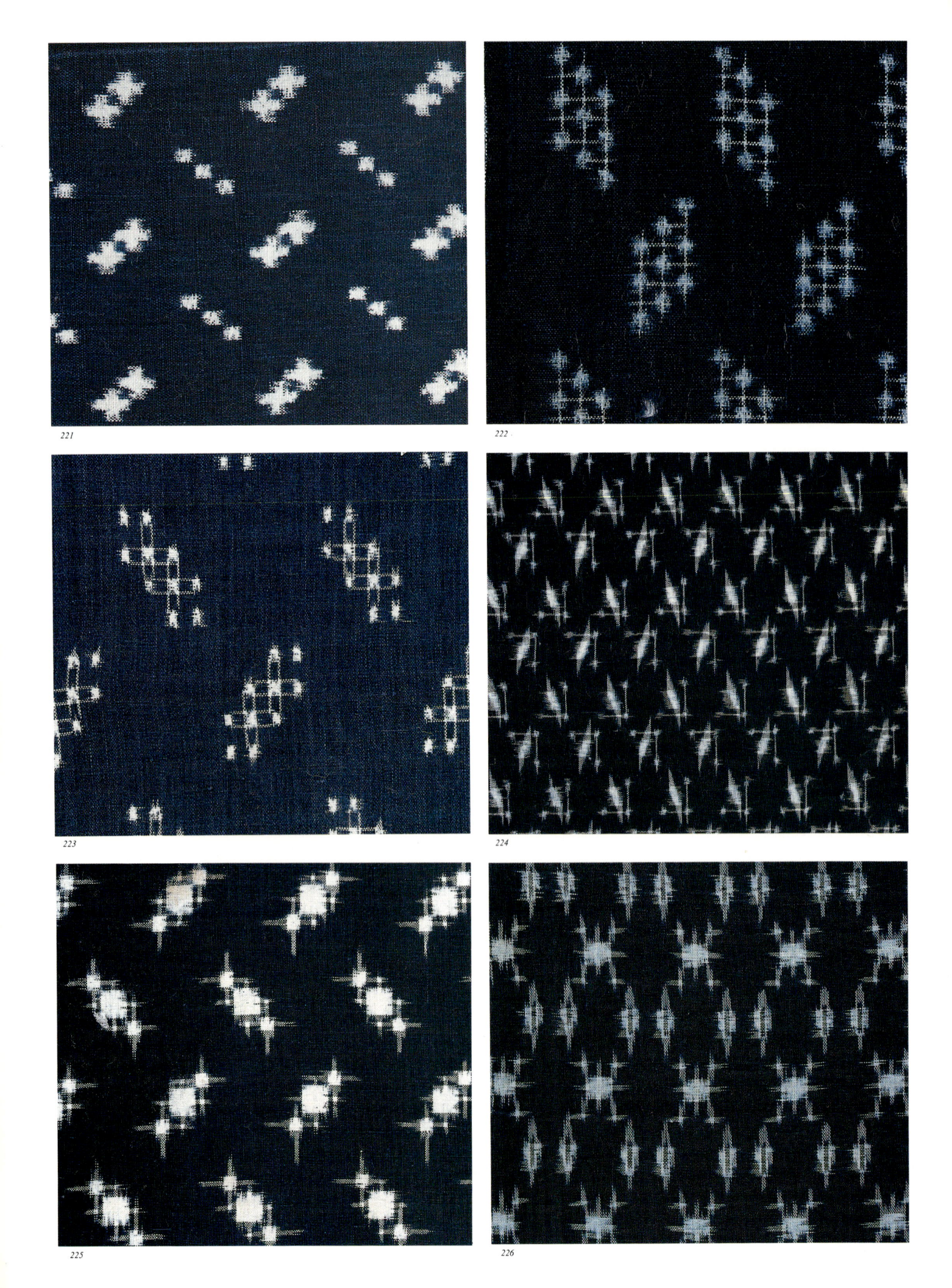

222

223

224

225

226

227

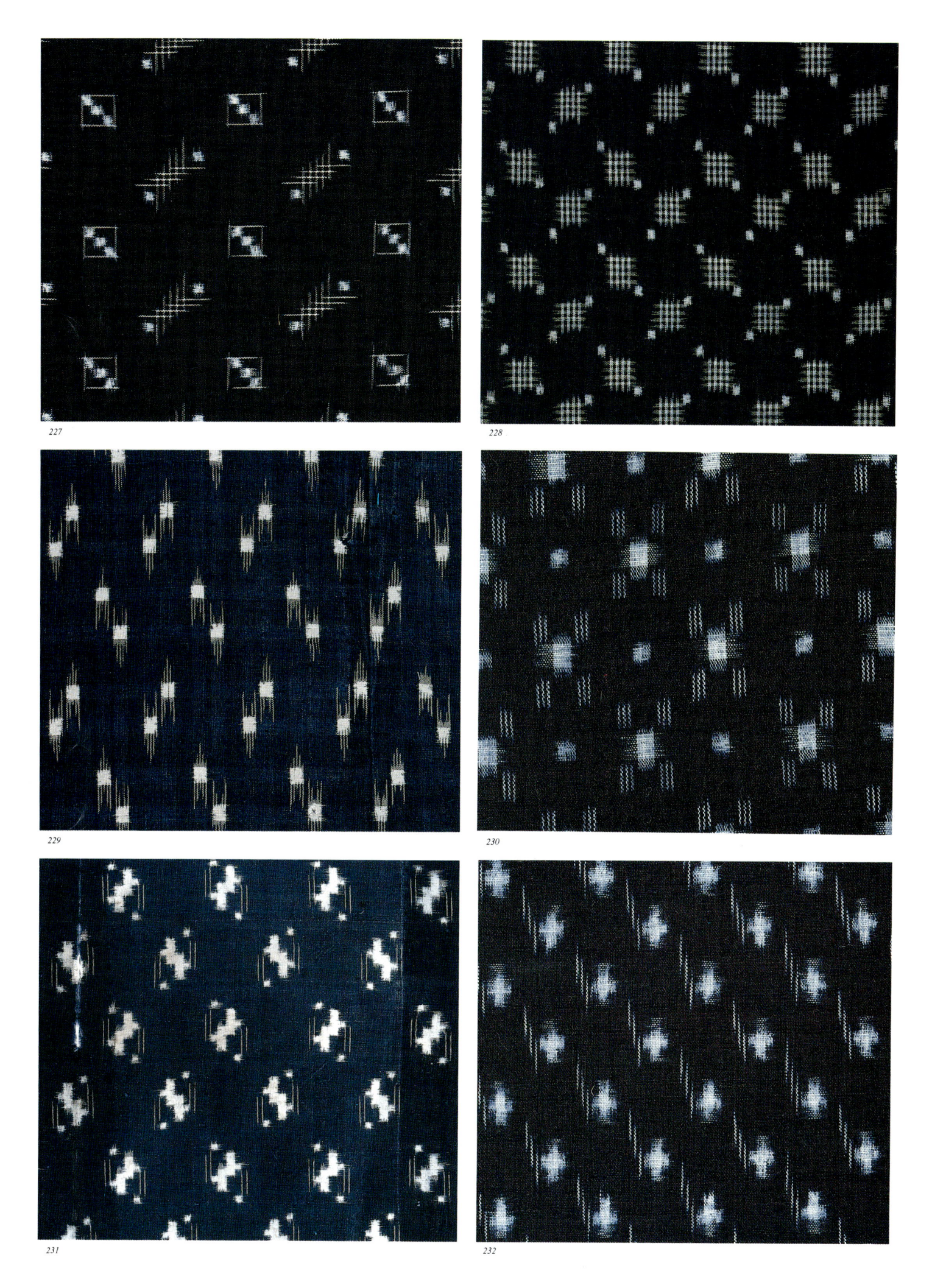

228

229

230

231

232

233

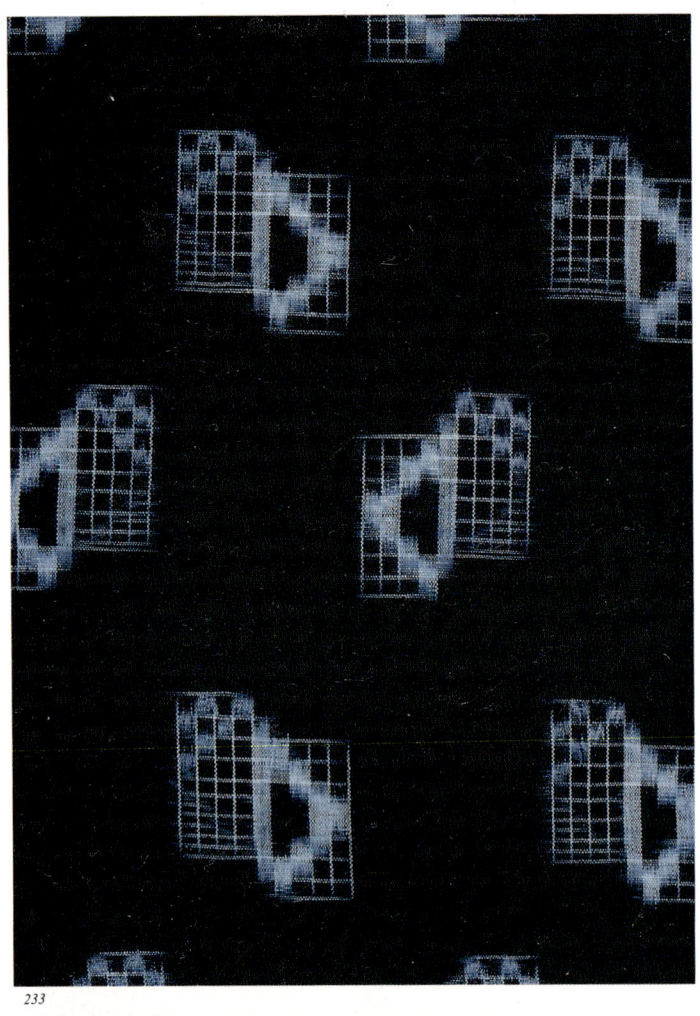

234

235

236

88

237

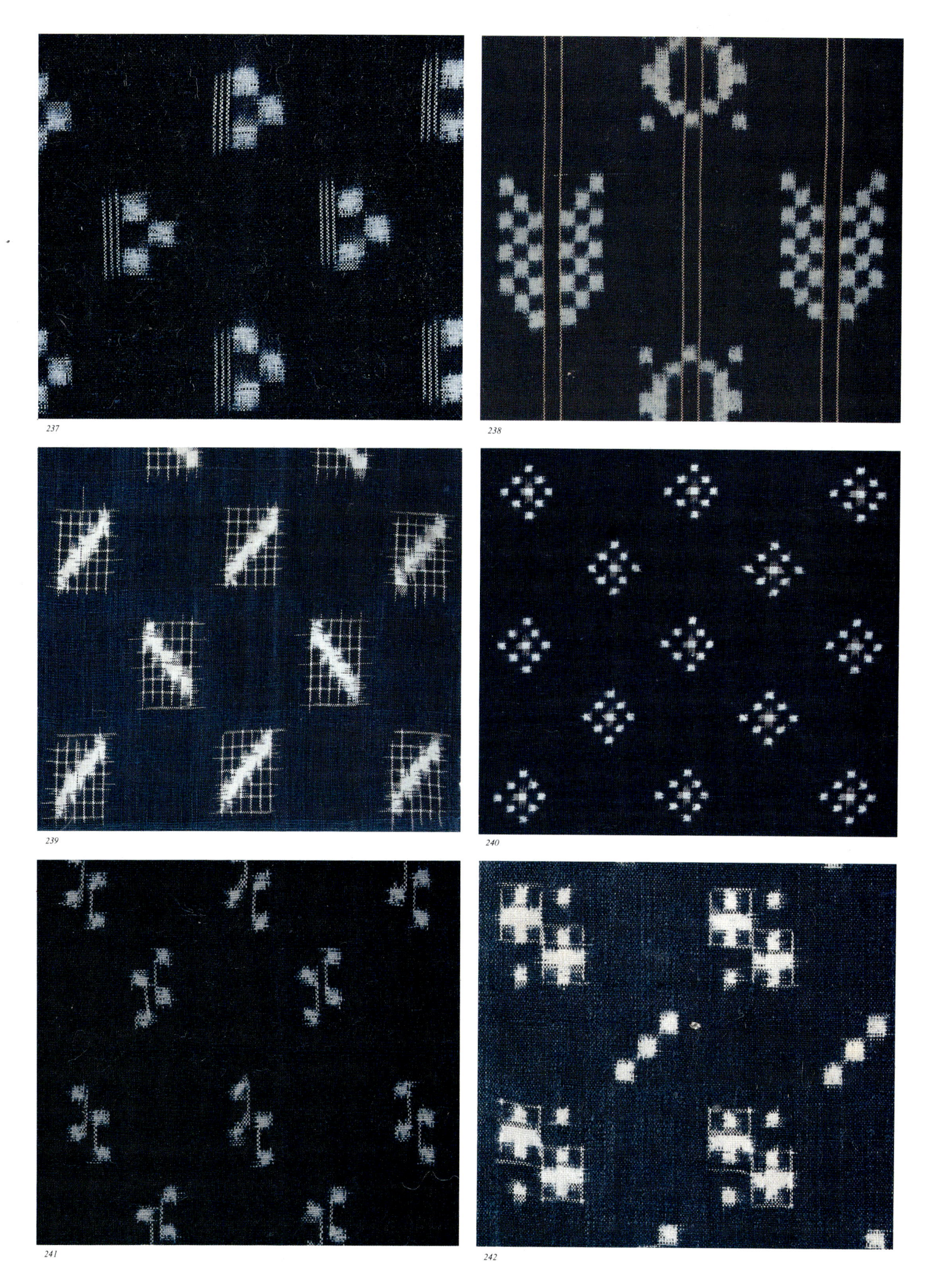

238

239

240

241

242

243

244

245

246

247

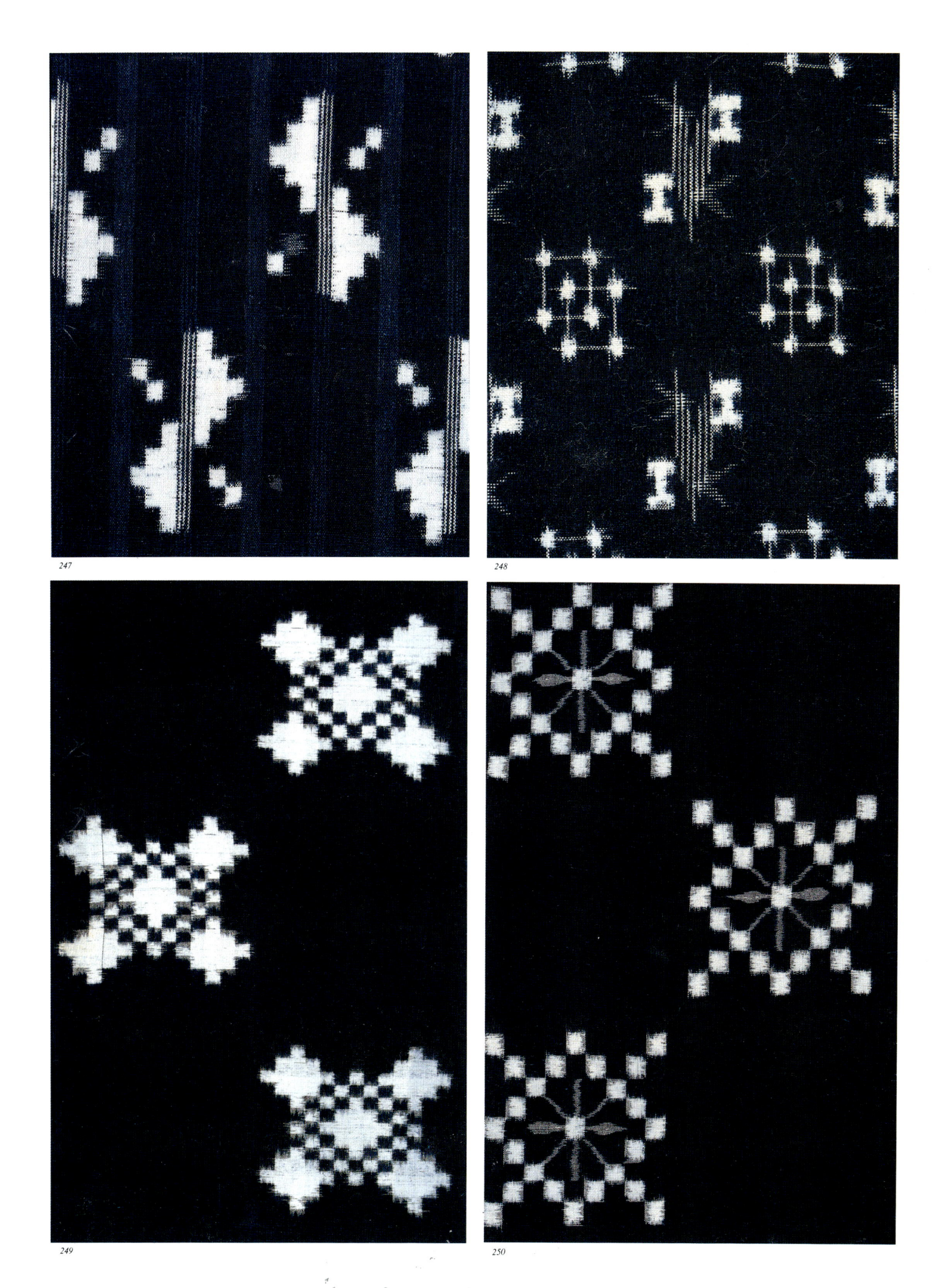

248

249

250

251

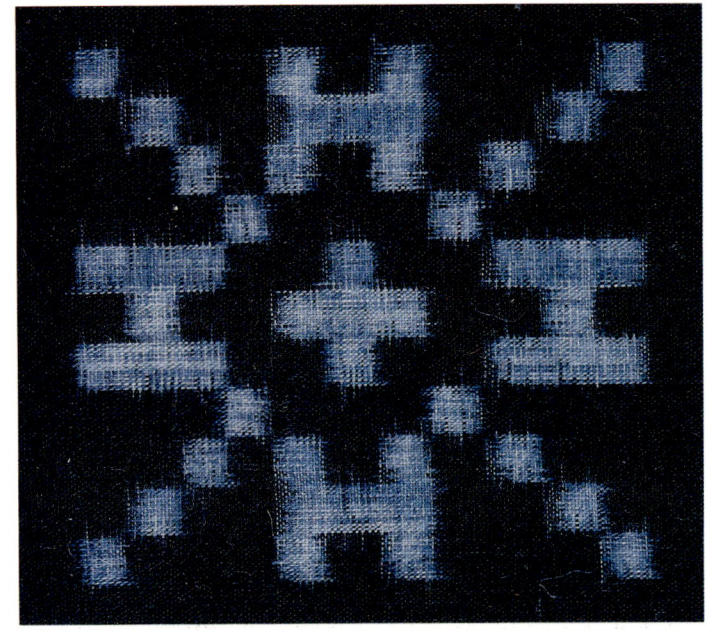

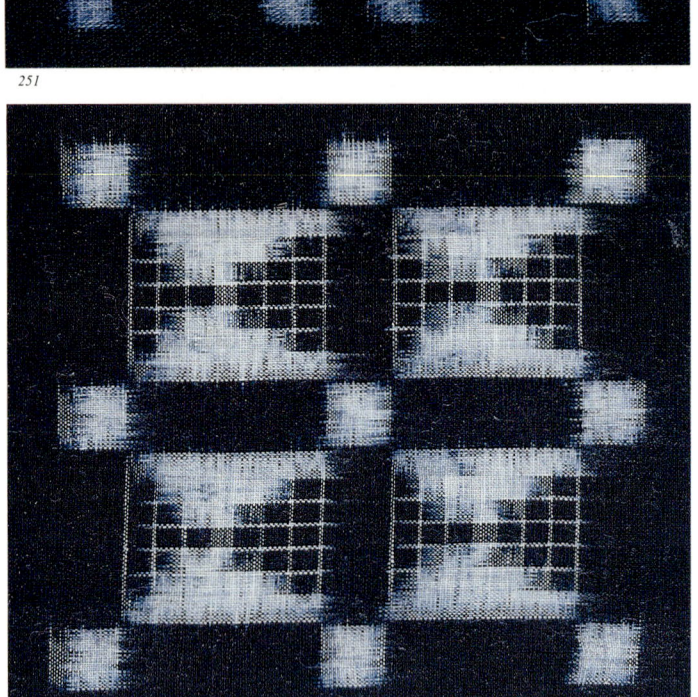

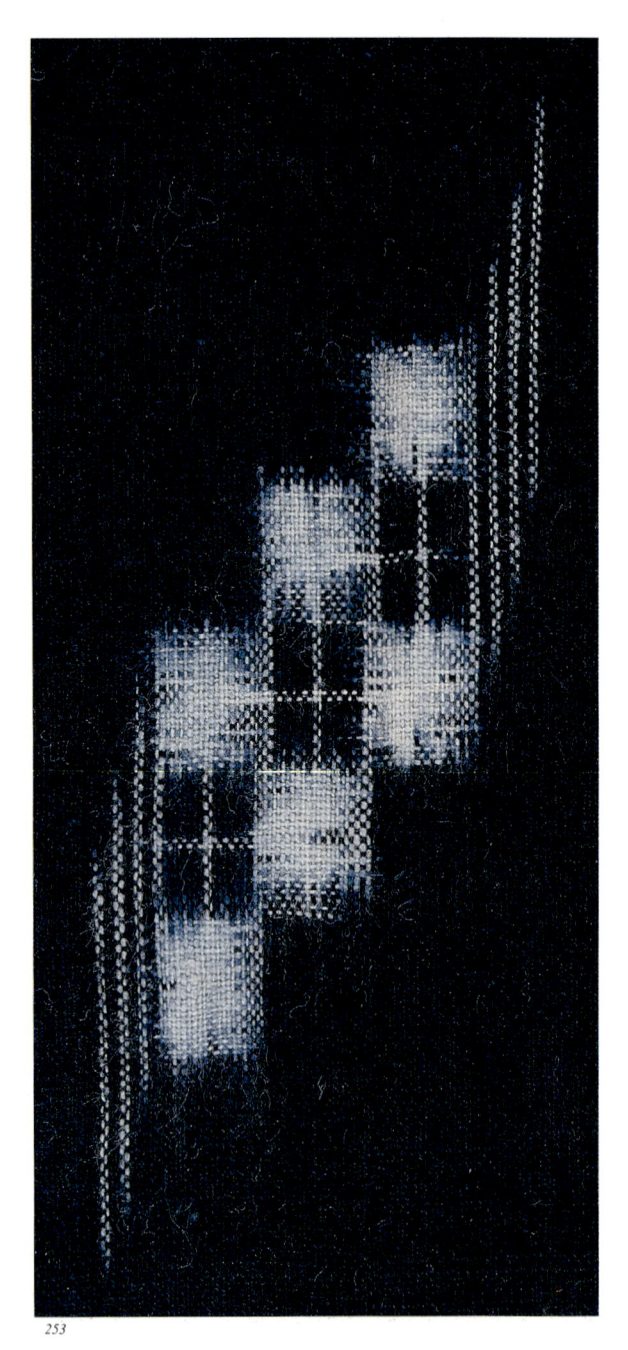

252

253

254

255

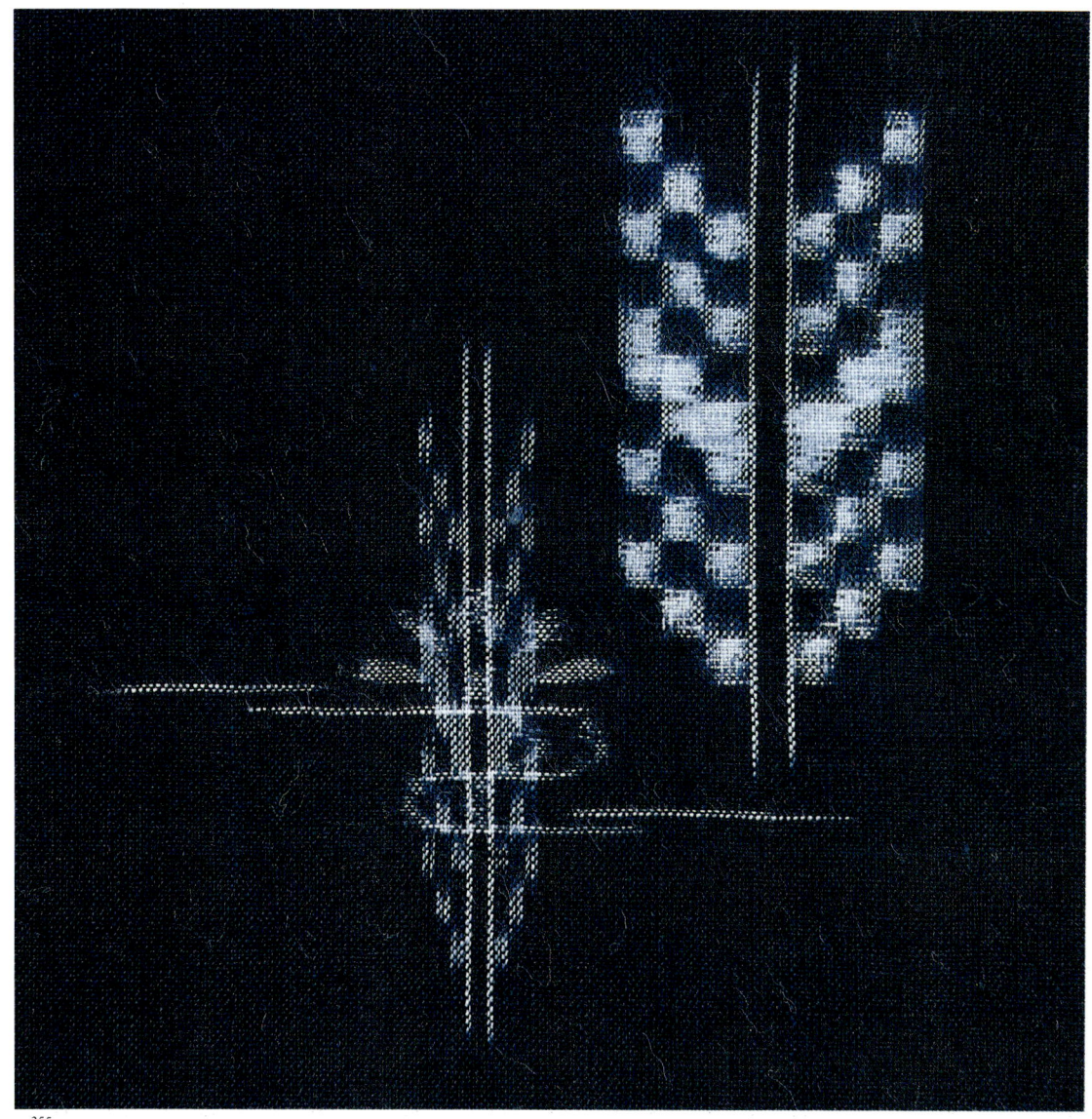

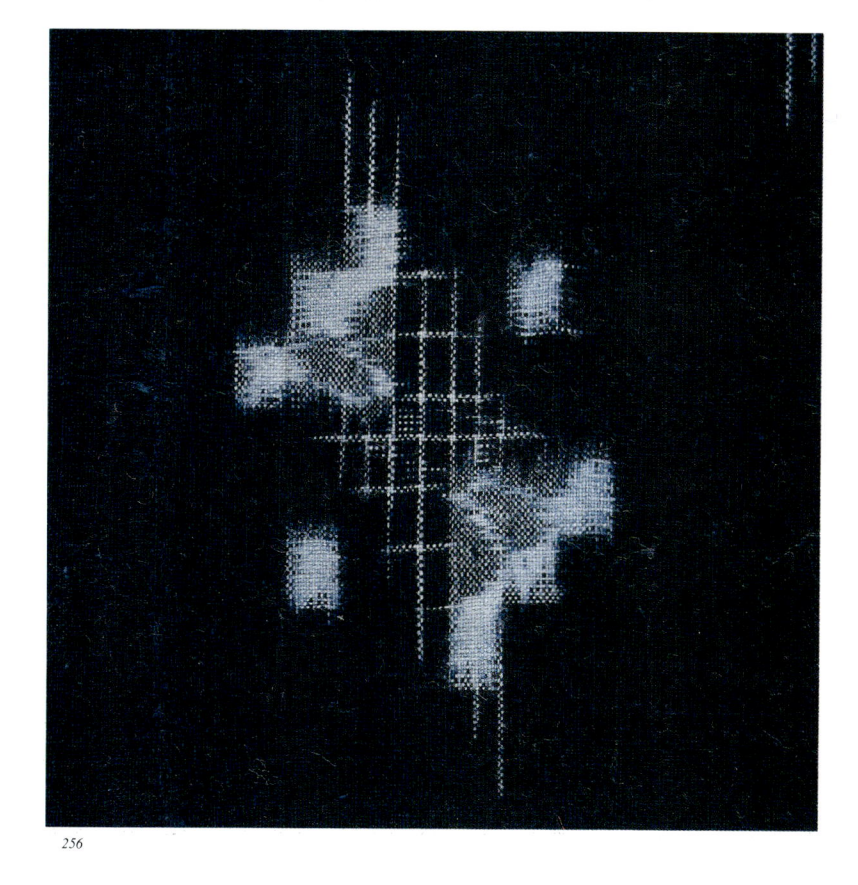

256

257

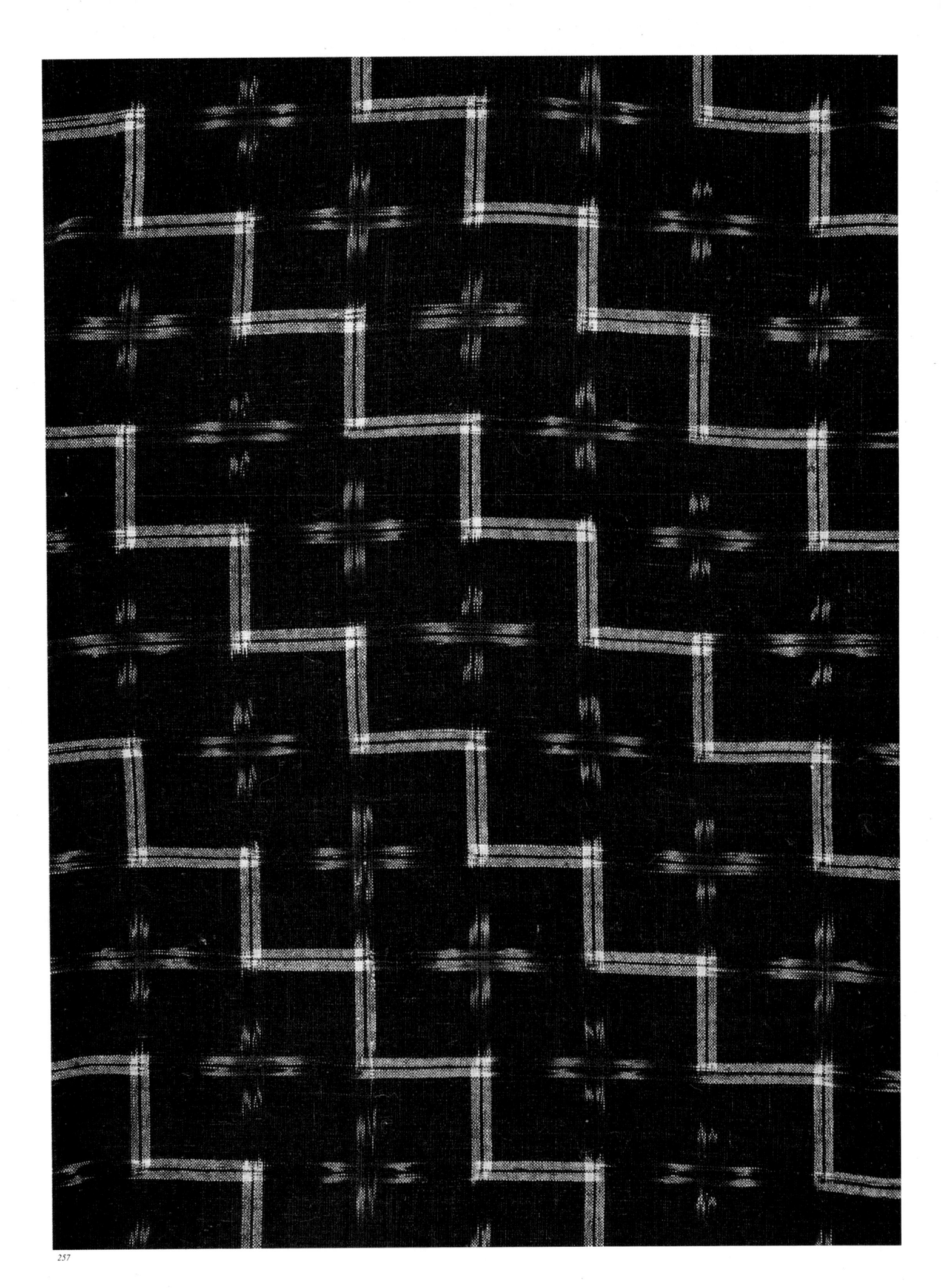

258

259

260

95

261

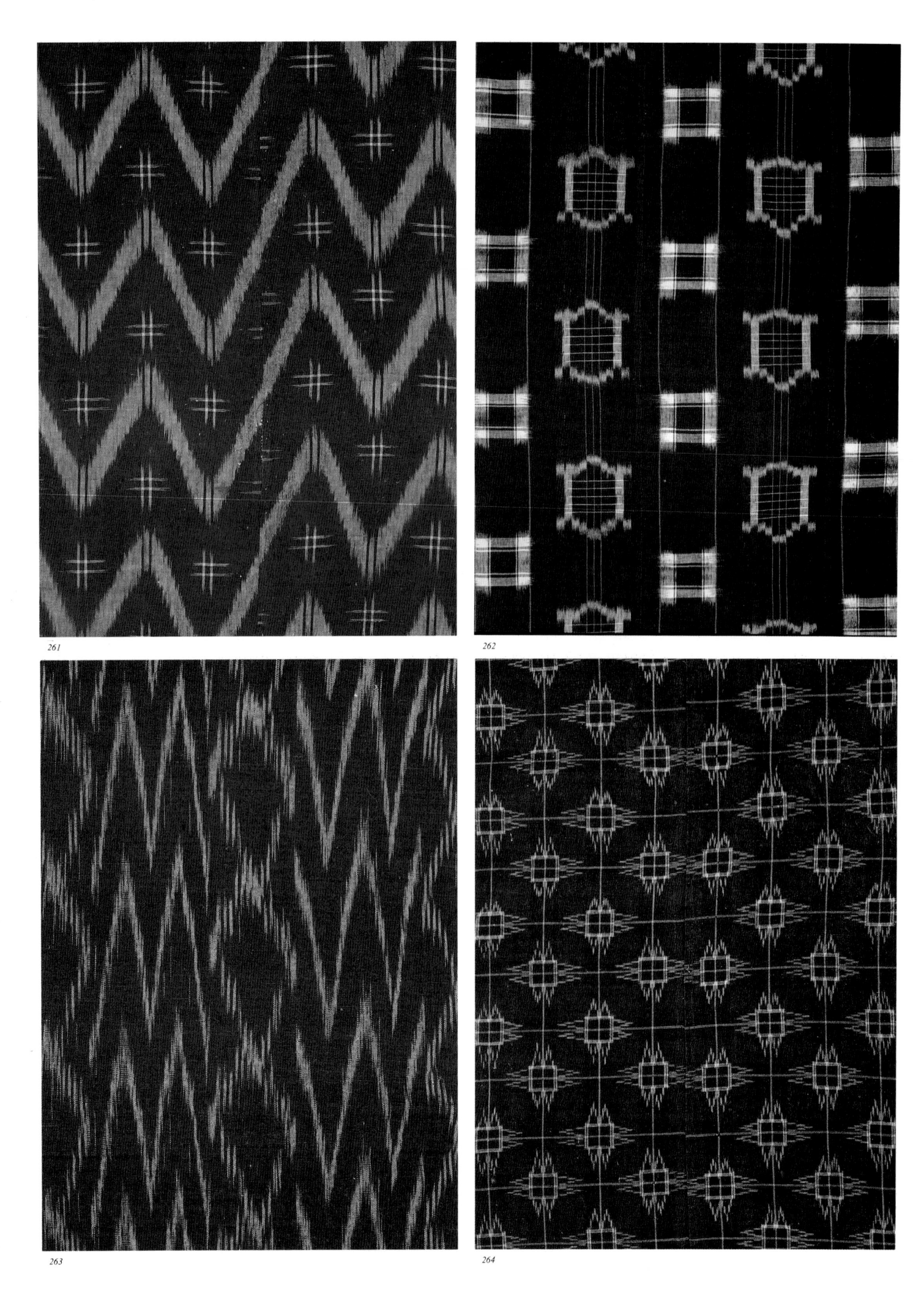

262

263

264

265

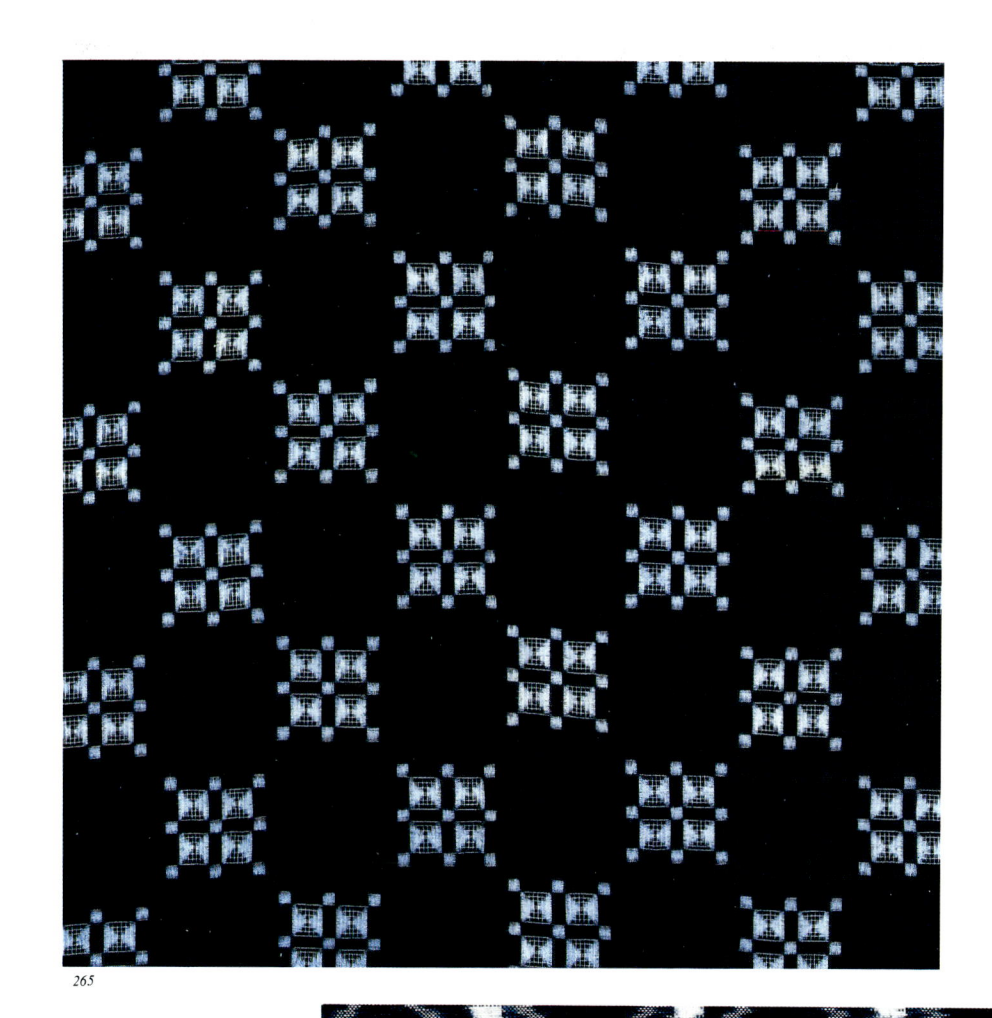

266

267

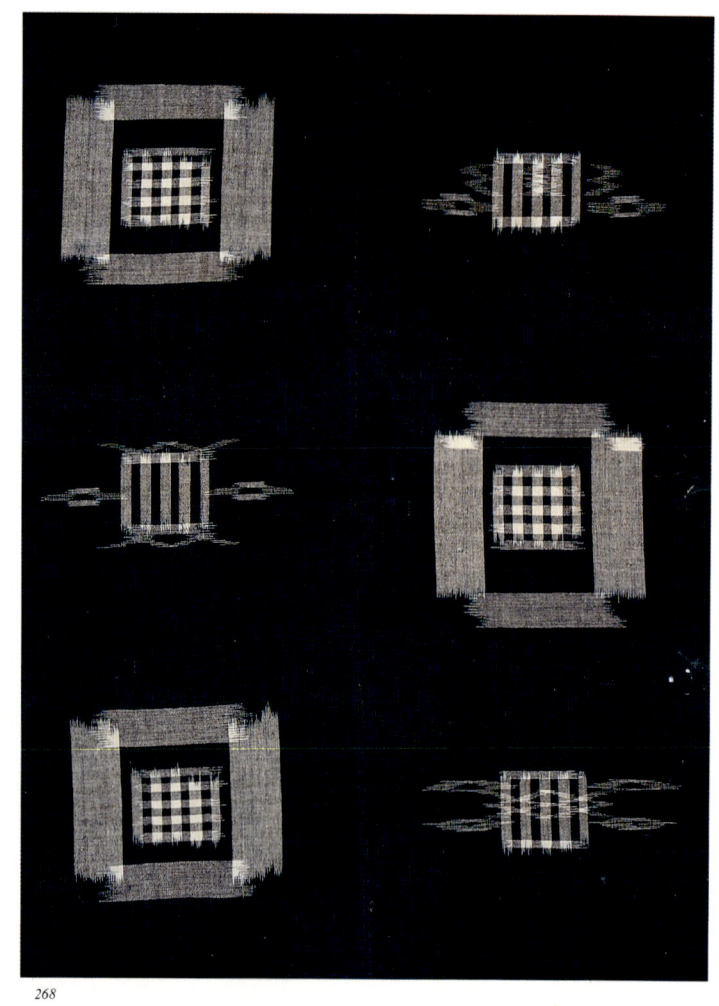

268

269

270

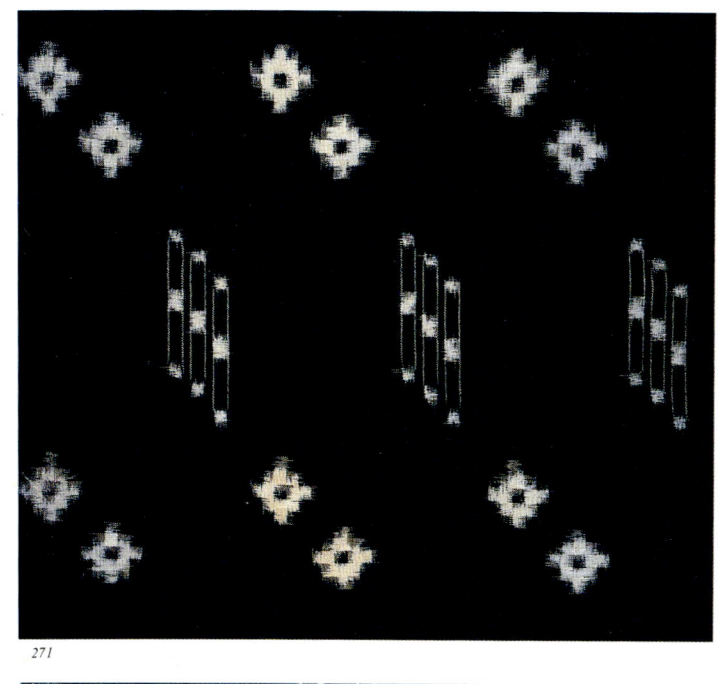

271

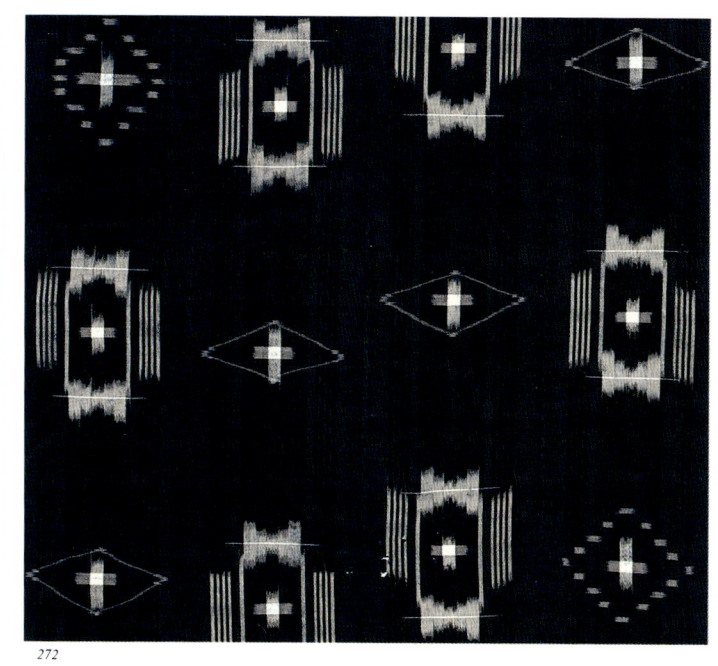

272

273

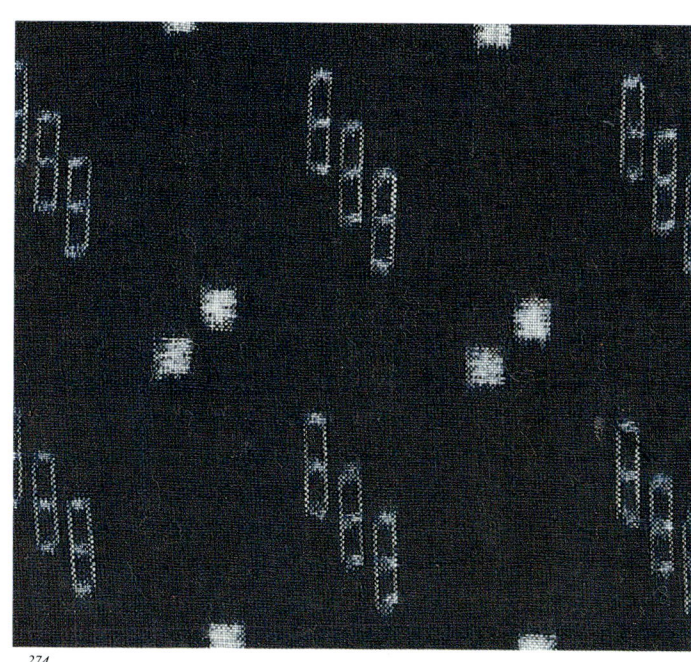

274

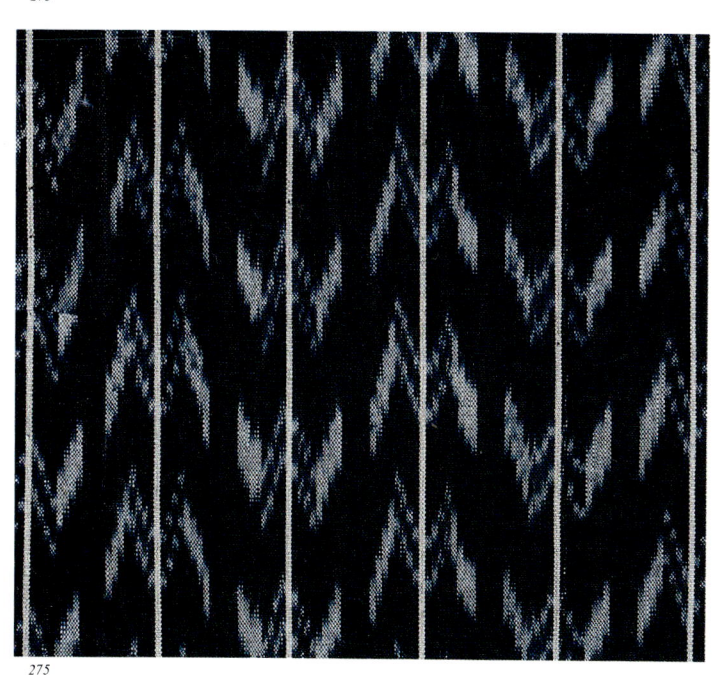

275

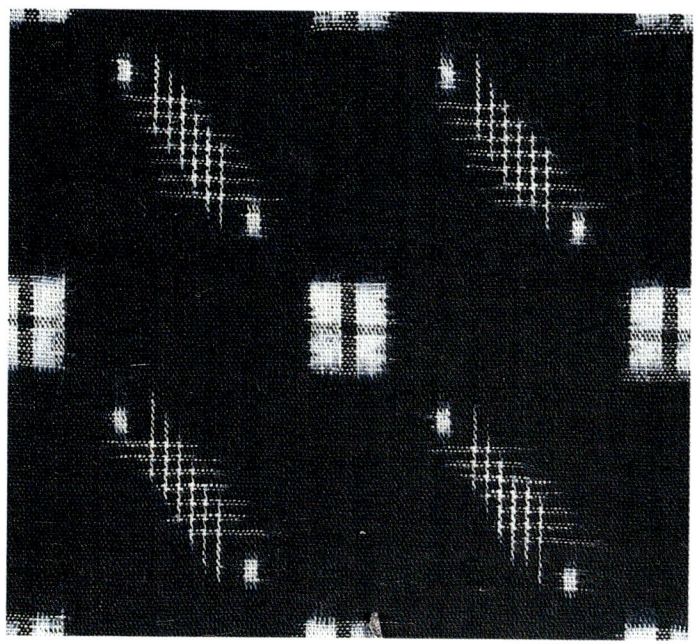

276

99

277

278

279

280

281

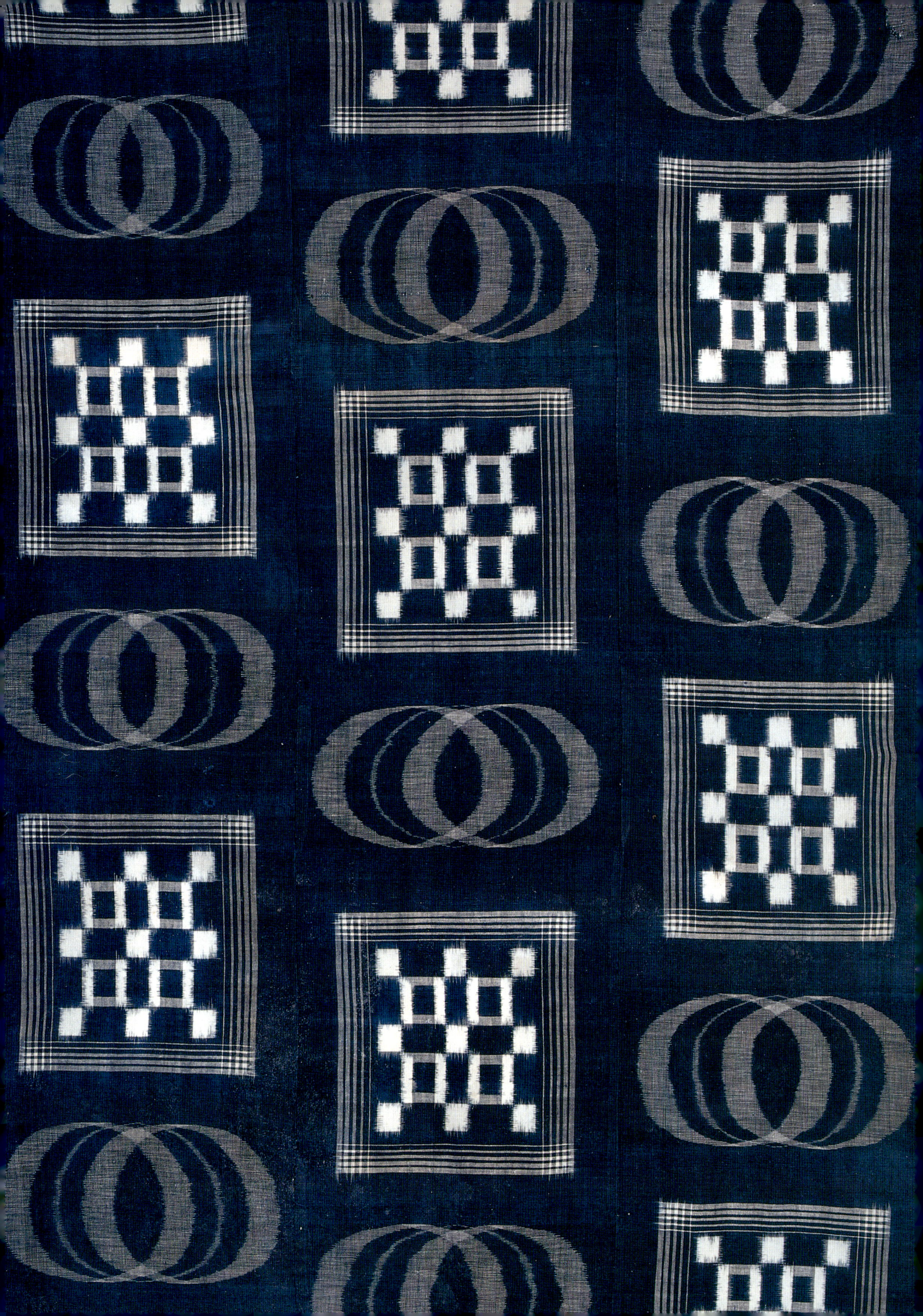

282

283

284

103

285

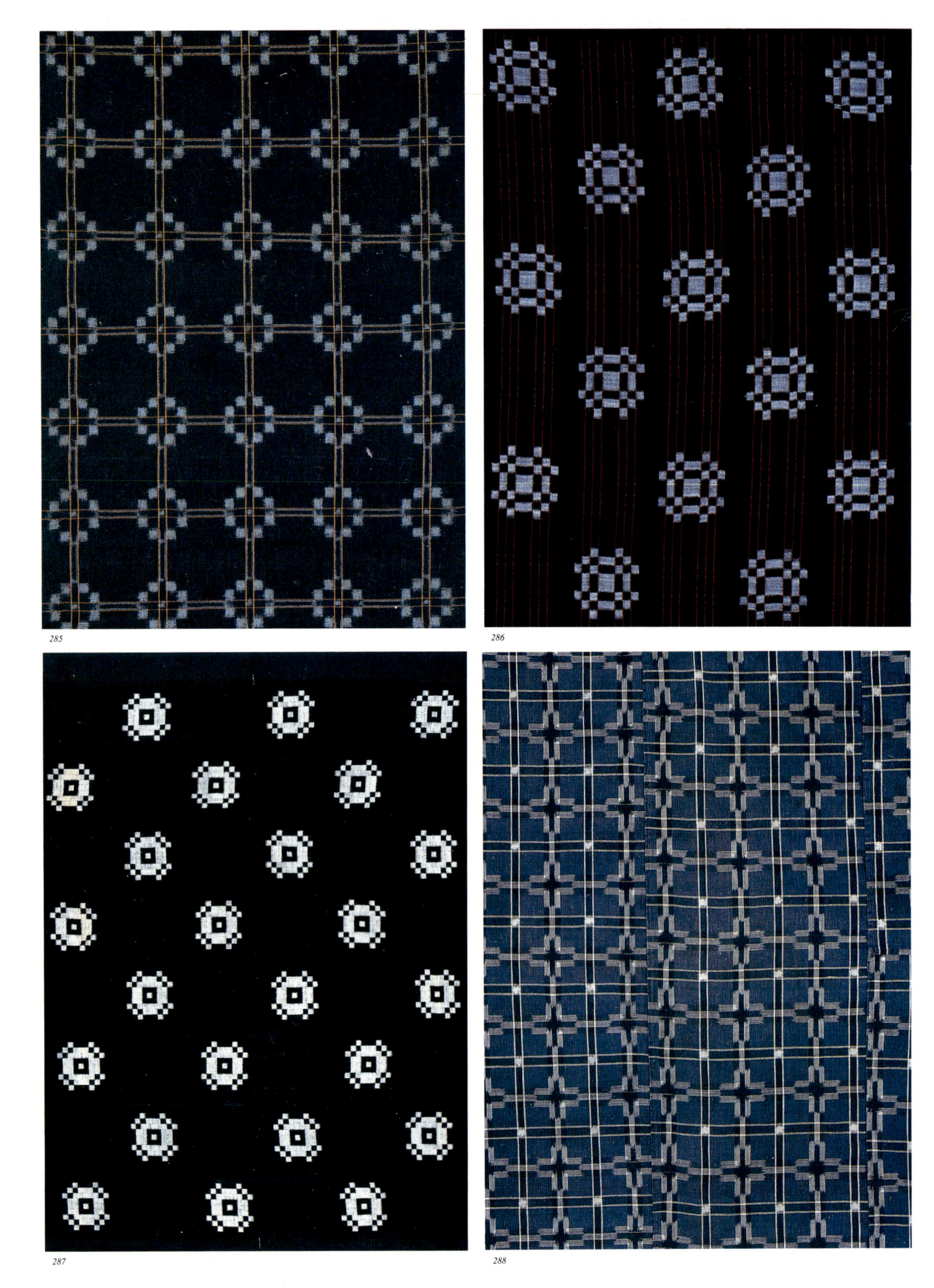

286

287

288

289

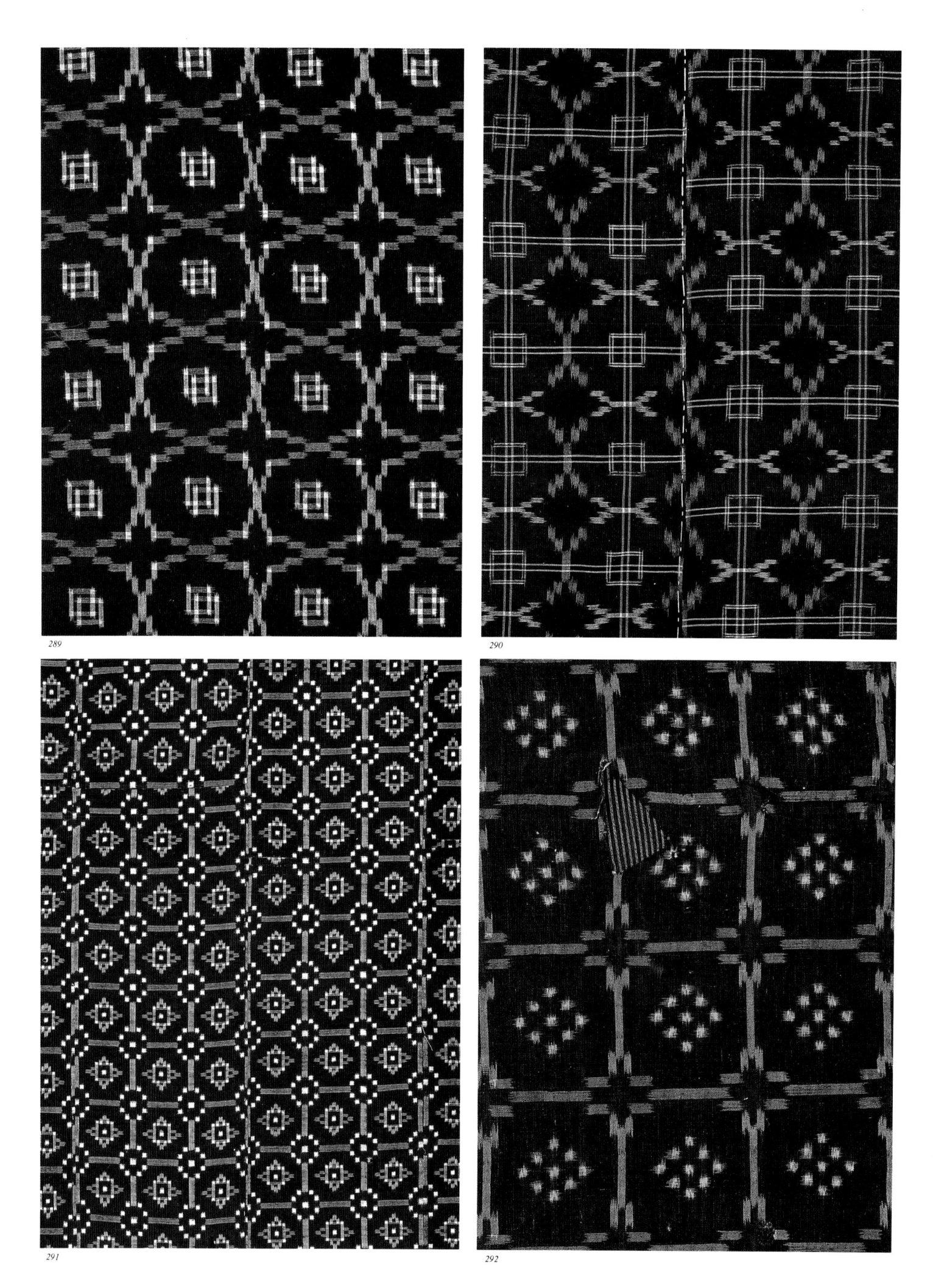

290

291

292

105

293

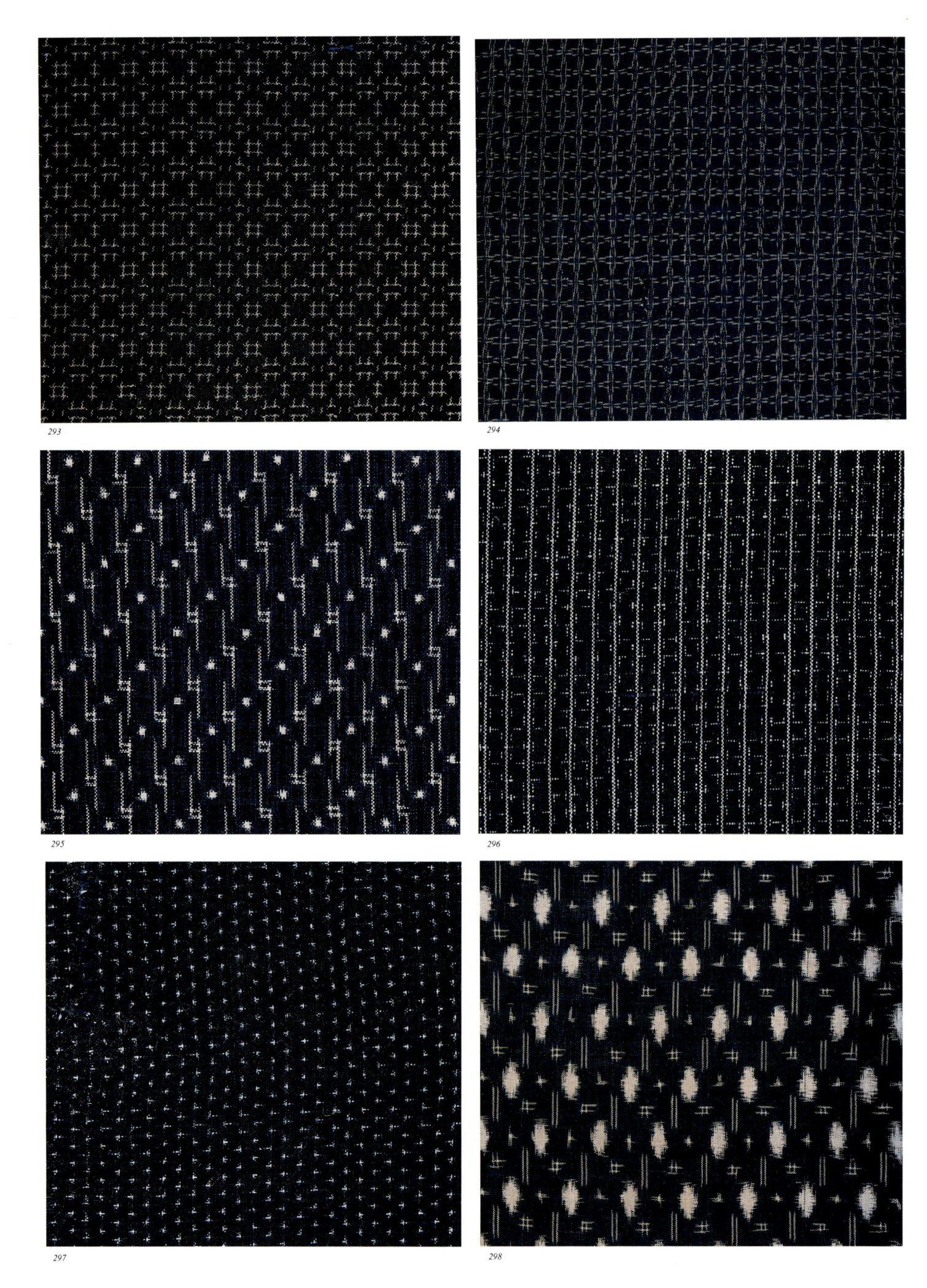

294

295

296

297

298

299

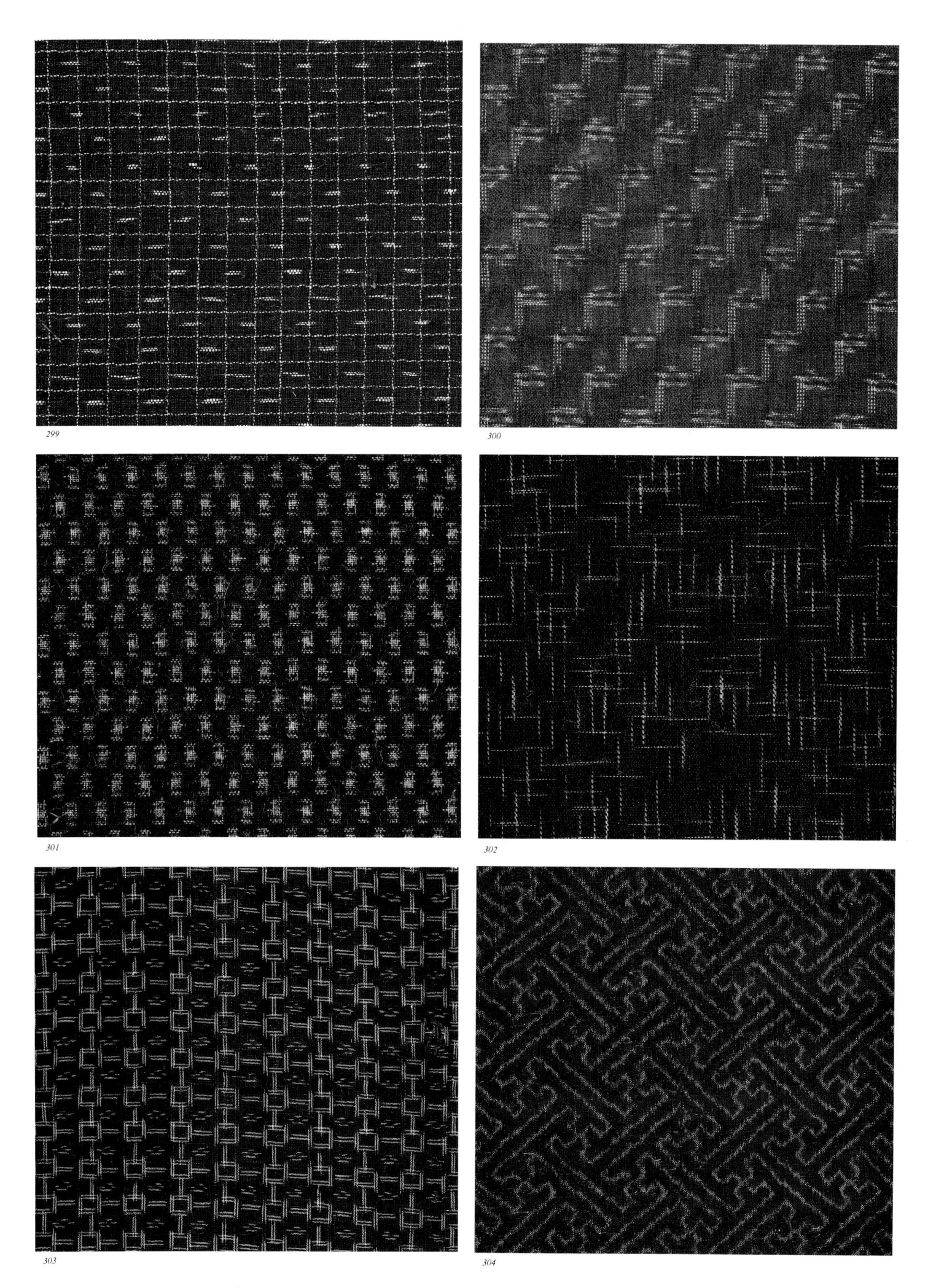

300

301

302

303

304

305

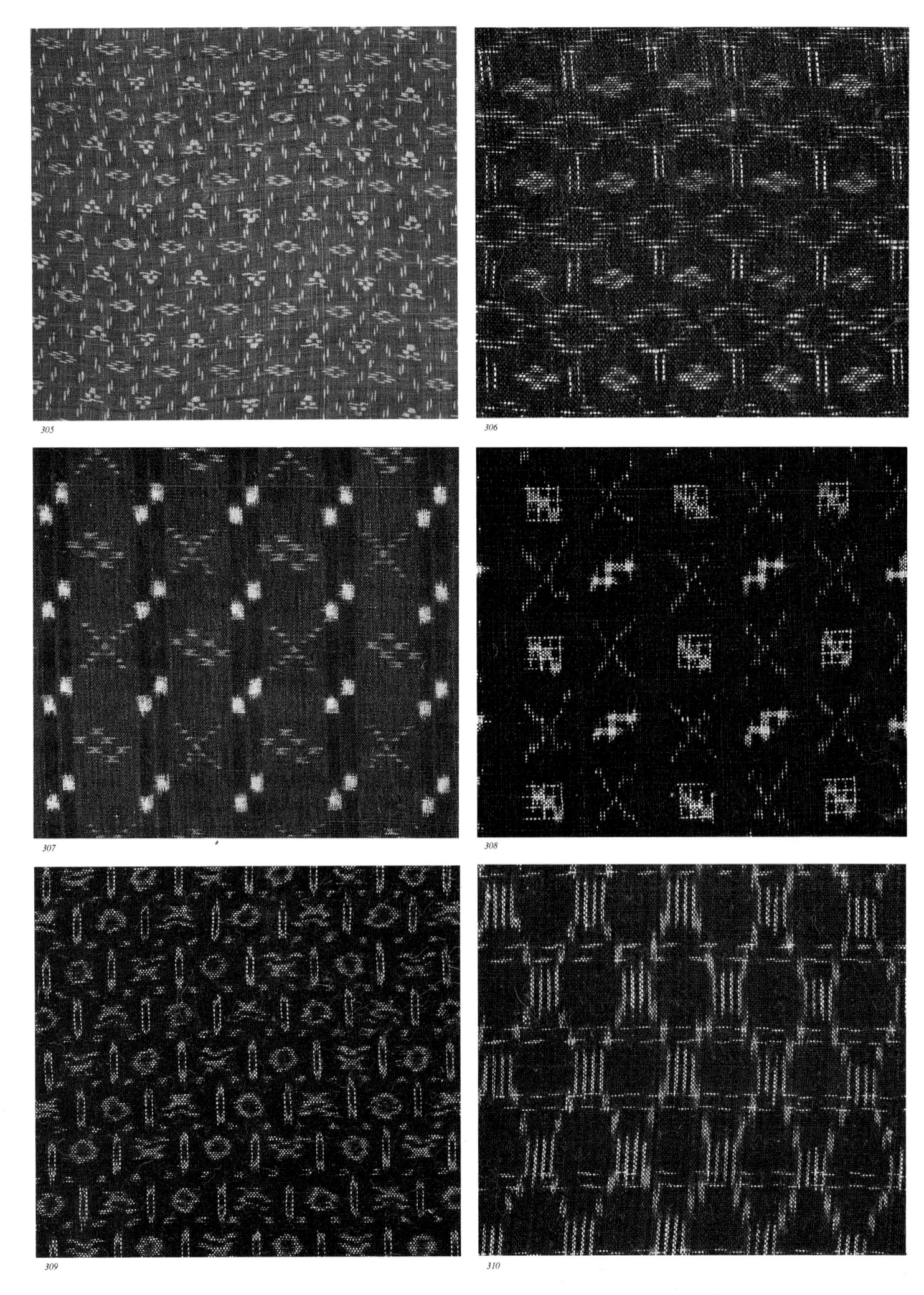

306

307

308

309

310

311

312

313

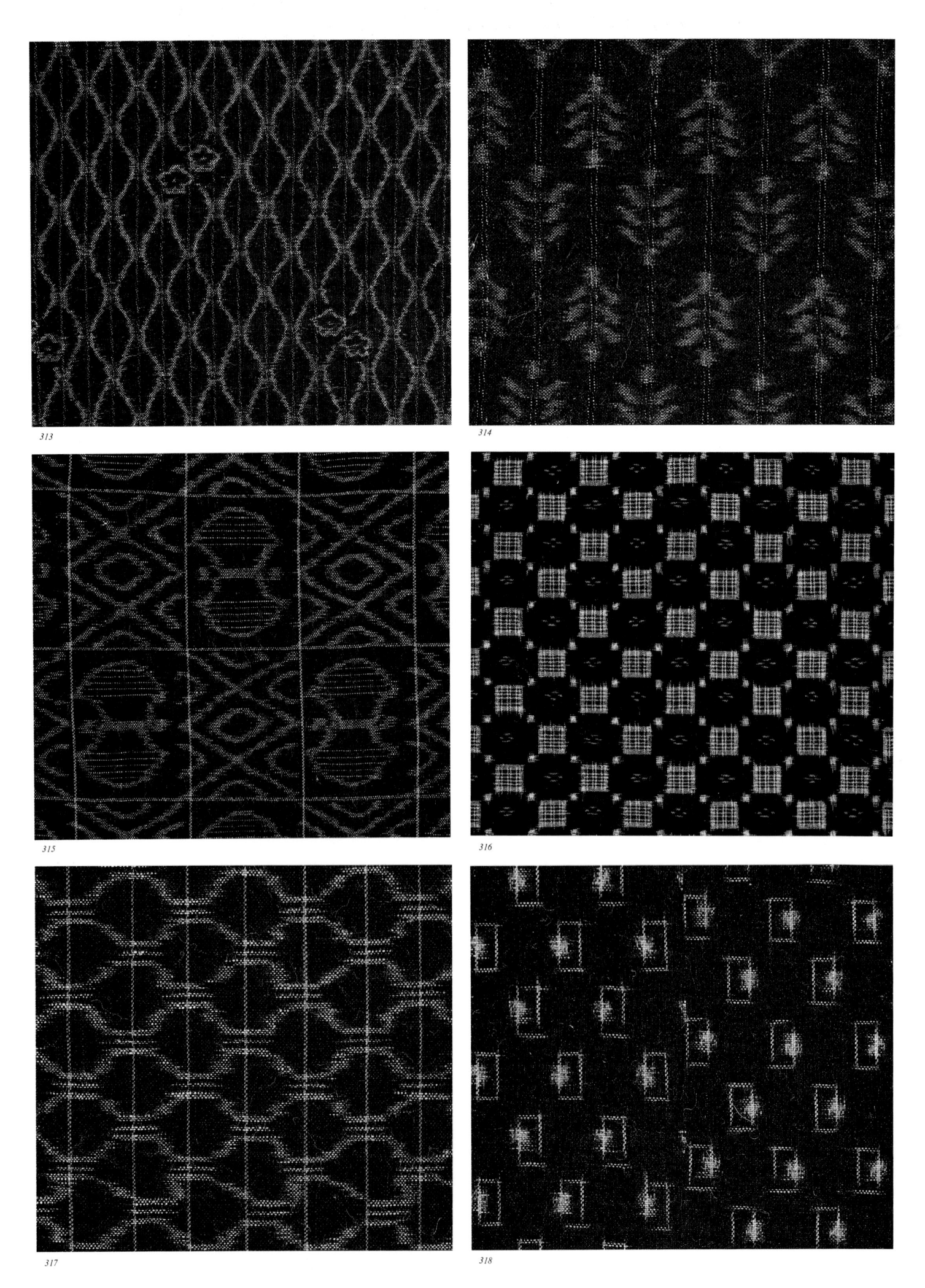

314

315

316

317

318

110

319

320

321

322

323

324